How to Live Life Victoriously

By Winifred Wilkinson Hausmann

Unity Books
Unity Village, Missouri 64065
1982

Cover photo by
L. LaMar Bell
Scene off the Oregon coast

Contents

Introduction

The Bible is filled with instruction — vital, living recommendations for everyday living that are as timely today as they were when they were recorded thousands of years ago.

Some of these instructions come to us in the form of definite teachings — clear, concise sentences that tell us exactly what we should do under given circumstances. Other instructions, though clear to those who lived in Bible times, must be interpreted in the light of present-day modes and customs.

Then there are the directions that are more subtle. These are in the form of stories, in many cases stories of people who actually lived and died, but who gave us a message in their words, their actions, their everyday living, and the vital choices of their lives which affected many other people to come. And, of course, there are the parables — stories told in terms of daily experiences and designed to present in a colorful way the spiritual teachings.

As we consider the instruction given in the Bible, our basic textbook, we can see that, regardless of what can arise in our present-day living, there is an answer. There is a definite, logical, and correct method for dealing with everything from troublesome people to our physical bodies, our financial affairs, and even our doubts and fears. The instructions are there. It is our job to find them and put them into practice in our lives.

This book is designed to help us discover those secrets of living. Putting them into practice is the work of the individual adventurer in Truth.

How to Make Right Decisions

Everyone wants to make correct decisions. We all have the deep down desire to do the right thing, to make those determinations that will open our lives to greater health, more harmony and peace, richer experiences of living, and those tantalizing goals of prosperity and success.

Even in our everyday activity, it is important to make the right choices in such simple matters as shopping for groceries or for clothes. We all want to choose the material things that will add beauty to our lives, increase our health, and bless us with comfort and a sense of security.

We can learn to make right decisions. There are certain rules we can apply to each choice, rules that will make us masters in the realm of decision making. Whether we are trying to reach some conclusion on a matter that represents a turning point in our lives or simply trying to choose new curtains for our homes, we want to be right. And we can be, by taking a lesson from a couple of people who lived (or perhaps only lived in an ancient allegory) long ago.

In this case, we can learn something about making correct choices by considering the choice made by the first man and woman in our recorded history, Adam and Eve.

First, let us consider the story of these two people who may remind us of ourselves.

Adam, of course, came first. He was put into a place filled with beauty. Everything was provided for his comfort and convenience. Here in the Garden of Eden *the Lord God made to grow every tree that is pleasant to the sight and good for food.* (Gen. 2:9)

But Adam was lonely. He had no suitable companion with whom to share this paradise. So God created a woman, Eve; and the two lived happily for a time in the Garden of Eden.

They had satisfying work and responsibilities. They were to care for the garden, and in return they benefited from its lavish production. There was only one limitation: God told them not to eat the fruit of the tree of the knowledge of good and evil, which was in the middle of the garden.

Having never known any place other than

the garden, perhaps Adam and Eve failed to appreciate the many blessings they had. As time passed, they had sampled all the usual fruit, and that tree in the middle of the garden began to look more and more appealing.

Perhaps snakes have wrongly been blamed through the years for Eve's temptation. Could it not have been that the serpent was simply the desire in her for sensation, for some thrill she had not yet experienced?

At any rate, she made a decision based on some sort of conversation in which it was determined that eating of the knowledge of good and evil was more important than the instruction God had given in the beginning. The voice of sensation became louder and louder; and the end result was that the woman not only ate the fruit, but she also persuaded her husband to eat; and from that day both their lives changed drastically. One decision not only affected them, but it also carried over to those who were to follow them.

The serpent of sensation won his point by declaring, "It's free," as he assured Eve: *"You will not die."* (Gen. 3:4) Had he used one of the modern slogans, perhaps he could more justly have said, "Eat now — pay later," because that's what they did.

Immediately after they made this decision,

they had to start paying. First, they felt uncomfortable. Knowing they had erred, they began to experience the pangs of conscience so strongly that they tried to cover up their wrong-doing. Also, thinking now in terms of good and evil rather than experiencing all good everywhere, they saw themselves as naked and attempted to construct some makeshift clothes of fig leaves.

But worse was to come. They couldn't continue to experience God's presence of life and love and joy in this new consciousness. And so, when their usual time of communicating with God came *in the cool of the day,* (Gen. 3:8) they tried to hide. But they couldn't, and in the long run they had to live with the results of the decision they had made in the heat of the day. The two were put out of the garden where all was so richly provided; and as long as they continued to think good and evil, they had to work hard for their living and suffer various other difficulties and challenges.

It may seem an arbitrary ruling that God made at this time. But actually, we find that after choosing to see all things in the light of a dual nature, Adam and Eve could no longer live in the perfect consciousness of harmony and beauty that the Garden of Eden represents. They had removed themselves from this state of mind, and so they had to leave the outer surroundings.

The first man and woman did not have to remain bound by their wrong decision, any more than we have to remain bound by our wrong decisions; but they could not experience the perfect awareness of the God presence until they were willing to change their thinking. And that was something they didn't choose to do.

As Unity cofounder Charles Fillmore explains: *Good and evil seem to be pitted against each other in the world, but it is not necessary for man to eat of the tree of good and evil; he need not have a knowledge of evil in order to realize the allness of good. If he follows God's way, which is to know the good first, last, and always, his mind will become so charged with good that evil will be to him totally unreal.*

So Adam and Eve made their first error when they stopped believing in God and His creation as all good. They had to stop listening to God, to stop accepting God as the one Presence and Power, Good, in order to obey their wrong impulses in the first place. That was their first mistake.

Then, instead of accepting the results of their own actions, they had to excuse themselves and look around for someone to blame. Adam blamed Eve; Eve blamed the serpent. And we

11

don't know who it blamed! But these early characters in our history set a precedent that survives. Individuals are continuing to look for someone to blame for their wrong decisions.

Obviously, if we want to make right decisions, we must stop blaming others for our trials, temptations, and difficulties, and start accepting the responsibility for our own lives and our own decisions. Only in this way can we prepare to receive God's guidance and the ability to follow through on right choices.

Adam and Eve made a third error that we cannot ignore. They continued to believe in good and evil! Their original error set them off on the wrong path; and instead of retracing their steps, they just kept going. Even their children were the expression of this, a continuation of the concept of confusion of right and wrong, good and error.

First, there was Cain, who expressed some good qualities, but who was so possessed by selfishness and anger that he killed his younger brother Abel. Adam and Eve, however, did make an attempt to get back to the spiritual plane and produced another son, Seth, who, in a sense, replaced Abel. But the two children carried on with varying success, as they represented two types of thinking. And so it went through succeeding generations.

In learning to work with spiritual principle to make right decisions, most people start out with some confusion. Frequently they ask, "How can I know when God is speaking to me? How can I be sure I am not just listening to my own thinking?"

This is a good question, and sometimes it is hard to determine just which thought is from God and which is from our mortal thinking. (The human race has become so entangled with the confusion of Cain and Seth.)

It is not always possible to know at first whether or not your guidance is from God. But if you feel good about it, follow up, and you will soon know; the results will tell you. When your decision is in agreement with the God presence and the God activity in your life, everything works out easily. But if you keep running into roadblocks, then it is time to take a second look. Go back and pray some more.

Adam and Eve had definite indications that they had made a wrong decision. First of all, they felt bad about it. They were uncomfortable. From a feeling of joy and peace, they had descended to uneasiness, fear, and guilt—emotions they had never experienced before.

Then they found they could not continue to think good and evil and live in the rich surroundings of the Garden of Eden. It was evident they had made a wrong decision.

Should this happen to us, we can return to our Garden of Eden consciousness by learning to open ourselves so completely to God in prayer that there is nothing else in our minds or hearts, just the awareness of God, All-Good. In this state of mind, this perfect awareness, we will always know what to do; and we will do it easily and in divine order.

But suppose we have not yet reached that state of mind? Then let us look at some definite rules, some "dos" and "don'ts" we can apply in making any decision.

Don't be in a hurry.

Mobs and their destructive activities taking place in the frenzy of excitement and mass arousal are a prime example of decisions made in the heat of the day. People who would normally act in an entirely different manner can sometimes be triggered into action that can cause damage. They do it under the pressure of anger, resentment, or some other heated emotion or sensation.

Adam and Eve show us that making decisions in the heat of emotion is not the wise way. In the heat of the day they decided to eat the fruit. In the cool of the evening they regretted their choice.

When we take a step at a time when we are

aroused emotionally, we will most likely do the wrong thing. The person who becomes angry at the boss and quits his job in a huff may later wish he had moved more slowly, or perhaps not at all.

An individual may be pressured into buying something by a salesman who arouses fear, saying, "If you don't take it now, it won't be here later." If we are working with God, trusting His guidance, we can be sure that whatever is ours by divine right will still be available in the cool of the evening after we have had time to think it over carefully and come up with a prayerful answer.

More than once my husband and I have confounded a salesman with this line by replying, "If it's ours, it will be here when we return." And if that was the right purchase for us, the item always awaited our return, even in times of seeming shortages and pressures to buy.

We have a friend who says she likes to pray about her decision after choosing a coat or dress that appeals to her. Laughing, she reports, "Nearly every time, when I go back the next week, the item is still there; and it's on sale!"

Don't try to force your own way.

Many people attempt to push through a decision by forcing other people to do certain things, by insisting things work out in a certain way, or by refusing to back down even when they know they are wrong.

Adam and Eve tried to force their good. They were so determined to have their own way that they simply ignored God's guidance and went ahead anyway.

That still, small voice within us may be muffled by our own loud, urgent, human demands. But when we listen, we can hear. And if we have to force, we can be sure that we are on the wrong track. God's way always works easily.

Don't be misled by the promise of something for nothing.

How many advertisements today are headed by that magic word "free," a misleading invitation to sign up now and pay later? Frequently it is only in the small, easily overlooked print that the prospective customer is told how much he will pay later.

In making decisions on purchases, we should always make sure we have read the small print too. The item may be free for the first ten days, or free with the purchase of a much more expensive product. Manufacturers are in business to make money; and, one way or another, advertised bargains are designed to benefit them financially.

Adam and Eve found that even the fruit of that famous tree was not free. For making their commitment to the wrong idea they had to pay, and pay dearly, when the time came. And so do we.

Even when it is something good that we want, we should make sure that we want to pay the price. If it is a matter of installment buying, we must determine our ability to handle it and our willingness to make the expenditure. There is nothing wrong with paying the price for something we desire, but we should do it with our eyes open and our minds receptive to God's guidance.

Even if seeking a better job, we must be willing to pay the price in increased hours, greater responsibility, or specialized training.

But when we are willing to pay the price, to do whatever is required of us, then we can have God's unlimited good poured out through our lives in ways even Adam and Eve never dreamed of.

Do choose that which is in keeping with your highest spiritual aspirations.

Wherever you are on the ladder of spiritual growth and attainment, you have some ideas about God and His goodness. You have some aims and goals rooted deeply in your spiritual nature. Start there in making your decisions. You do not have to compromise with error in order to express Truth!

If the decision you are making seems to combine good and evil, remember the first man and woman who got into trouble by trying to make those two ideas work together.

Choose goals that are in keeping with God as love, health, life, strength, prosperity, success, and happiness. Then let your decisions as to steps to take to reach these ends be based on your present understanding of God's principles.

Many times people try to compromise with life by ignoring their true desires and working "for a living." Where there are true talent and ability and a deep inner urge to express them, there is a way. Faith-filled, love-based prayer will reveal the way. You will never be truly successful in anything that is not in keeping with your deepest ideals and goals in life.

Do make all decisions "in the cool of the day."

In the Garden of Eden story, evening was the time when the first man and woman talked with God, or, as we might say, had their regular prayer time. After they decided to think good and evil, they began to be concerned about the time when they would have to communicate with God; and they even felt they could hide from Him.

"The cool of the day" is the time when we are calm, peaceful, relaxed, and open and receptive to God only. Only at this time and in this way can we be sure of coming to right answers.

No matter how pressed you may be, take time to become so still that you may meet the Father walking in that perfect awareness within you. There you will hear. There you will know. There you will make the right decision.

Do be flexible, leaving the final outworking up to God.

Sometimes even our best spiritual understanding cannot show us the final result of a decision we are making. Maybe we have limited ourselves by expecting a certain outcome. But God always knows so much more than we, even with our best insight, can see. So let us leave everything open for His plan to come forth.

We do this by being willing to change if God says to do it differently. Acting on our best spiritual understanding, we are to go forward as far as we can see with faith in the all-providing God. But, just in case God has some happy surprise that He hasn't yet revealed to us, let us always end our prayer, "This, or something better. Thank You, God." Thus, we are receptive to any change in plans that may be necessary for the fulfillment of a greater plan than we can project at the present time.

Do be willing to try again.

That first couple made a decision that was destructive but not irrevocable. Since those early days, we (mankind and womankind) have been working our way back in consciousness to the original awareness of the universe of all good which God created in the beginning.

In the past, we may have made decisions in our lives that led to destructive results, broken dreams, and shattered illusions. But even these decisions are not hopeless. Negative results can be changed by a change of heart and direction.

As we recognize mistakes of the past, we take the first step to correcting them; and, by applying these rules for making right decisions, we can so attune ourselves to Divine Mind and awaken our ability to receive God's guidance that our new decisions will negate the old results and repair broken bridges. They are our way to return to the Garden of Eden consciousness, where all is peace and harmony; and prosperity and health are the perfect outworking of being perfectly attuned to God only.

How to Have Total Healing

Healing is always possible! No matter how extreme the healing need, there is an answer. There can be a way. Universal healing principles, as taught in the Bible, apply not only to conditions of the physical body, but also to healing of the mind, the emotions, and the affairs.

No matter what the ill that afflicts the body, it can be resolved. No matter what disturbance wracks the mind, it can be alleviated and then dissolved. No matter how deep the hurts or how serious the problems in human relationships, they too carry within them an answer that is right, good, and complete. Finances can be healed, and so can personality problems.

In fact, God's way is the way of health, wholeness, harmony, prosperity, order, and justice; and it is God's particular pleasure to work in and through our lives to correct anything that appears to be wrong, and to establish for us greater joy and well-being—and richer living than we have ever known!

Not only can our minds, our bodies, and our affairs be healed, they can be healed completely! We do not have to settle for halfway measures when we are dealing with God and cooperating with His laws. Jesus said: *"You, therefore, must be perfect, as your heavenly Father is perfect."* (Matt. 5:48) What He promised, we can bring about, when we are willing to trust God and to cooperate with His laws for healing that is complete and permanent.

Jesus was continually teaching these laws as He went about healing the multitudes. Rarely did He perform a healing without giving some insight into the principles He was using. Those who desired to learn the way of healing were continually being instructed by the Master.

Never did Jesus indicate in any way that the cure had to be incomplete. Always He worked with the individual until the healing was finished, and He even gave instructions for maintaining the good result that had been achieved.

Jesus never settled for halfway measures. He never indicated in any way that any condition could possibly be "incurable." With Him and with those who were willing to trust in the spiritual power with Him, it was healing—all the way. There were no exceptions.

We too can experience complete healing, strength, vitality, health, and wholeness when we learn to break out of old habits of illness and fear and old willingness to settle for just so much of God's good. We are limited only by our ability to accept the gifts God is giving us now; and we can have complete healing of mind, body, and affairs by increasing that ability, by learning to know with our whole being that only the best is good enough for a child of God!

As we approach the question of healing, let us not settle for halfway measures. Let us not just hope to "get better," but let's go all the way. Let's claim the divine perfection that is our right as children of God, the perfection Jesus prescribed for us, His followers in Truth.

We increase our ability to receive by learning to live by the principles of healing as taught and demonstrated by Jesus. They are as vital and real today as they ever were, and the everyday story of Jesus' life is full of the teaching.

Consider the day Jesus was walking beside a pool near the sheep gate in Jerusalem. This pool was well-known in the area as possessing properties of healing, and many people with physical difficulties of all sorts congregated there seeking a miraculous cure.

The legend was that an angel troubled the water of the pool from time to time; and after the water was disturbed, the first person to enter the pool would be healed. Needless to say, this possibility of an instantaneous cure attracted people with all sorts of diseases and difficulties. No one knows exactly what happened to the water of the pool. Quite possibly the agitation was caused by an underground spring. But at any rate, the people believed; and whenever the waters rippled, someone was healed— the first one to get there. Each healing increased the faith in the miracle-working power of the pool, and it became a system that always worked for the believers.

Jesus, with His great insight into the hearts of others, stopped to speak to a man lying beside the pool. There must have been some reason why He chose this particular person from the group of invalids lying around the portico waiting for the opportunity to enter the troubled water and be healed of their infirmities.

Jesus stopped and asked this man, who had suffered from some sort of illness for thirty-eight years: *"Do you want to be healed?"* (John 5:6) A ridiculous question? No, because He could only work with someone who truly desired wholeness.

Thinking in terms of the only hope for healing that he recognized, the man replied: *"Sir, I have no man to put me into the pool when the water is troubled, and while I am going another steps down before me."* (John 5:7) His whole concept of the possibility of healing was centered on the idea of getting into the disturbed water. But somehow he was responsive to Jesus' tremendous consciousness of God's healing power, because when the Master invited: *"Rise, take up your pallet, and walk,"* (John 5:8) he did; and he was healed. He didn't just limp away a little better for the healing treatment; but he picked up the bed on which he had been lying and walked off, completely well.

The man had one more lesson to learn. He had to keep the healing he had accepted, and Jesus found him later and told him how to do that. But first, let us look at the lesson of healing taught in this earlier encounter. There are some definite instructions here for anyone who wants healing of mind, body, human relationships, or affairs. We can see exactly what we shouldn't do, and what we should do, if we want healing that is complete and lasting.

Don't wait for something outside yourself to heal you.

Look for an excuse, and you can always find one! But excuses don't work miracles. They simply delay the time when we accept the good God has for us.

Many people make the mistake of looking to some source outside themselves for their help. They may set their own conditions, saying, "If only . . . then I could be healed." And so they wait. Perhaps the man in the Bible story had become accustomed to seeing others healed but not really expecting that he could be the first one in the water. It was probably not unpleasant to lie there in the cool shade during the day, perhaps receiving alms from passersby. If he had been first in the water, would he really be ready for the healing? Or was it easier to wait and let someone else go first?

Perhaps it never occurred to him to ask that if one could be healed on entering the water, why couldn't the second man also receive his answer? And the third? And the fourth? Why just the first? After all, faith determines the healing. Had just one person set a precedent, there could have been a whole new pattern for restoration of health to these people.

What does this tell us? That we don't need to wait for someone or something outside ourselves to restore our minds, bodies, and affairs to the perfection God implanted in us from the beginning.

A father and mother, much concerned about

their child's listlessness and lack of appetite, took her to doctor after doctor seeking a cure. Finally they found one wise man who wrote out a prescription that brought about her healing. He wrote, "Take this child to the park four times a week and play with her." The child's need didn't lie in the realm of medical science, but the healing came about easily when her own spirit of joy was awakened. The cause for healing was within her all the time. It simply had to be called forth.

We too have within us the potential for the healing of any ill of mind or body. But when we look to outer effects and hope for someone to do for us what we are unwilling to do for ourselves, we may spend our days waiting and wishing, as did the man beside the pool of Bethesda. And in the long run, we must see that wishing and waiting are not the way to healing.

So, instead of looking to someone or something outside us to bring about our healing, let's see what we can do. This story gives us definite instructions.

Do decide that you really want to be healed.

There is a price for healing, and we must be willing to pay the price before we can bring about complete and lasting results. We may find surcease from an ailment; but if the deep down desire for wholeness is not there, sooner

27

or later something else will trigger a recurrence of the difficulty, be it mental, physical, or in the realm of effects in the world.

Let's look at our story again. Here was a man who had been accustomed to a certain type of life. Each day he came to lie by the pool. While others worked in the hot sun, he languished in the shade. Undoubtedly he received both sympathy and alms from passersby. Healing, when it came about, would bring tremendous changes in his life-style. He would have to pay the price!

When he was well, certainly he would have no excuse for lying beside the pool. He would have to join the workers of the world, perhaps learning a trade or even doing menial labor. He would have responsibilities and would at the same time be giving up the comfort of sympathy from the others he met. Before speaking the word of healing for him, Jesus had to be sure he wanted it. That was why He asked: *"Do you want to be healed?"* (John 5:6) It was something for the man to think about!

We too must ask ourselves this question, and answer honestly. Do we really want to have a particular relationship with another person healed—enough to pay the price? Are we willing to accept the responsibilities that will come with wholeness of our physical bodies? How do we feel about giving up the satisfaction of telling others our troubles? (We must, if we want to get rid of them.)

Doctors increasingly point to the importance of the patient's attitude in healing. Many physicians prefer not to operate on people who are expecting to die. More than one has expressed a special joy in working with the optimistic, happy individual who prays and anticipates healing with faith and expectancy.

"Do you want to be healed?" It is a question we must consider carefully and answer honestly before we go on to the next step. If we are to have total healing, permanent wholeness, we must be sure we are mentally ready to receive it.

Do act on faith.

God works with us to restore mind, body, and affairs; but He can only work through us. In most cases, even prayer is not enough. We must also take those outer steps that prove our faith.

This doesn't mean doing something ridiculous like walking on a broken leg just to dare God to make it well. It does require that we do what we can to help ourselves. After preparing mentally for our healing and making our contact with God (as the man in the story made his contact with Jesus), we must listen to His guidance and then follow it all the way. While we are doing our part, God can do the rest; but He simply can't heal us if we are unwilling to help ourselves.

If we desire healing of our finances, God may guide us in finding a job; but in most cases He will not simply drop a packet of money in our laps. He has many channels, and He has many ways of bringing about healing. All are available to us when we pray. But He will tell us just which one is right for us at this particular time. And when we follow the direction of Spirit, our healing comes forth in divine order.

In the Bible story, the ailing person started out by making excuses. He would be healed if he could get to the water first, but obviously he wasn't able to do that; so healing simply wasn't possible, according to his thinking. Had he continued to complain and to blame, he probably wouldn't have heard Jesus' instruction. We too must overcome the temptation to make excuses, to blame our troubles on others, and to complain about conditions if we want to hear the inner Voice that will tell us what we must do. It can only speak to our conscious minds when we are still, when we are listening. So let us turn away from excuses and complaints and give God a chance to speak in us.

Jesus gave three instructions to the invalid beside the pool. All of them undoubtedly seemed difficult, if not impossible; but the man, through faith, responded anyway and received his reward of wholeness.

The first command was: "Rise." If we are to be restored to God's perfect idea, we also must rise out of thoughts of lack and limitation. We must lift up our vision to a new and greater idea of life and living. We must stop feeling sorry for ourselves. We must stop blaming others. We must be up and about our Father's business, the business of learning and growing as children of God. We must rise.

Then we must obey the second instruction: "Take up your pallet." When the man picked up his bed, he made a decisive gesture that showed that he was through with illness and the symbols of it. In taking this step, we may first be guided to simply stop talking about whatever appears to be wrong. We can't associate with illness or inharmony in our conversation and at the same time erase it from our lives. When we learn to listen to God, He will instruct us clearly as to how we are to take this step. He will tell us exactly what to do to remove from our thoughts and our environment the symbols that are perpetuating whatever is wrong.

Then Jesus instructed him to walk. It sounds like an easy thing to do, but not for a man who hasn't walked for thirty-eight years. In effect,

Jesus was simply saying, "Be well. Accept your healing now." And the man did. Immediately when he obeyed, he was made whole.

We too can have healing by obeying these instructions, sometimes as quickly as the man in the story achieved his overcoming. But if we would keep the good result, we must go one step further.

Effect whatever changes are necessary in order to keep the healing.

The man who had been cured was so excited that he scarcely knew what had happened to him. A crowd gathered around, and he told about the Man who had spoken to him; but he had no idea who He was. Later, when the initial furor was over and the man was by himself in the temple, Jesus found him and gave him a further lesson. He said: *"See, you are well! Sin no more, that nothing worse befall you."* (John 5:14)

Difficulties are rooted in error thinking and negative feeling. It is not enough for us to have an outer cure. We must have the inner cleansing of mind and heart if we are to have permanent healing. There is no other way. Every healing need has a cause in the thinking-feeling nature. If we would keep a changed effect, we must remove the original cause.

Jesus recognized the error in the man's mind

and, as on other occasions, He pointed out that the old "sin" (wrong thinking) must be corrected, or some other effect would be projected into visibility.

Unity cofounder Charles Fillmore, speaking of sin, explains:

Sin is man's failure to express the attributes of Being — life, love, intelligence, wisdom, and the other God qualities.

Sin (error) is first in mind and is redeemed by a mental process, or by going into the silence.

Through the Christ Mind, our sins (wrong thinking) are forgiven or pardoned (erased from consciousness). When we have cast all sin (error thought) out of our mind, our body will be so pure that it cannot come under any supposed law of death or corruption.

A complete change of mind is the only way to total healing, as Jesus pointed out on more than one occasion. But He also pointed out repeatedly that healing is always possible.

We can start where we are by applying the principles He taught as we understand them now. Then, by listening and learning, by believing and acting on our faith, we can be healed. And we don't have to settle for halfway measures. It is our business to be strong, vital, alive, spiritual, beautiful, and free. And by patterning our thoughts and feelings always on the highest and the best, we can fulfill our purpose.

Total healing is the first step in our spiritual journey toward the fullness of joy promised all through the Bible.

Health, well-being, wholeness, harmony, and life are our divine right. By doing our part, we can have them now!

How to Prosper Under All Circumstances

Right now, this moment, you are rich! It doesn't matter what you have or don't have in the way of material possessions. It doesn't even matter that you may think of yourself as under-privileged or poor. Nothing can change the truth that at this moment you are rich, because you are a rich child of God!

You are rich in joy, love, and peace. You are rich in opportunities. You are rich in ideas. You are truly wealthy in all that matters most, and you can have all the material possessions you are willing to claim from the storehouse of God's abundance.

You are a rich child of God right now!

The Bible is filled with references to the affluence that has been prepared for us as God's children. Over and over the Scriptures tell us that we have a rich inheritance which is ours for the claiming.

David, the shepherd boy who became king, sang: ... *I have a goodly heritage.* (Ps. 16:6)

Isaiah the prophet predicted wonderful blessings as *"the heritage of the servants of the Lord."* (Is. 54:17)

Jesus, too, spoke in terms of our inheritance. In a parable, He told of the king who invited those who had made right use of their powers to *"inherit the kingdom prepared for you from the foundation of the world."* (Matt. 25:34)

Peace and plenty are predicted for the righteous—those who make right use of their abilities—and for those who serve God.

Many people have felt that the Bible's promises of affluence and joyous living apply to some faraway time and faraway place; but, as we learn to apply the principles of prosperous living as taught in the Bible, we find that we can experience the joy and affluence of the kingdom right where we are. The secret is to find the kingdom, the God consciousness, within ourselves. When we do, we will attract into our lives all that we need to be prosperous and successful. Not only that, but we will also experience the inner joy and peace that enable us to enjoy the good we attract in outer ways.

There is no particular virtue in being poor. As one wealthy businessman commented, "It may not be any easier for a rich man to enter the kingdom of heaven, but I certainly don't think it is fair to claim that it is easier for a poor man."

Once we establish in our own thinking the idea that God intends us to be happy and successful, we will find that we do not have to be limited by circumstances, education, or background. And we will discover the true joy and fulfillment that come through the claiming of our rich inheritance now.

We can be happy. We can be respected in our communities. We can have peace and harmony in our human relationships. And we can attract all the outer wealth we are able to use. When we discover this, we will be through with excuses forever! We will know continually that we are rich children of God; and each day will be a thrilling and satisfying experience in prosperous, successful, spiritual living.

Let us understand that prosperity is not a matter of owning certain possessions. It is, rather, the development of a rich consciousness, a continual awareness of God's presence as our unlimited supply. When we have this constant acceptance of Spirit as our instantly available answer to every need, then it will not matter how outer circumstances change or what lack and limitation seem to be expressed in our lives or in our world. We will always have plenty, and we will always come through every challenge richer than we were before.

Consider the story of one of the wealthiest, most powerful men in the Bible—Joseph.

As a boy, Joseph was by no means poor. His father Jacob was a wealthy patriarch, richly blessed with flocks and herds as well as a large household. Although Joseph was not the eldest son, the one who would normally inherit his father's estate, he was Jacob's favorite. So he was pampered, petted, and generally favored above his eleven brothers.

His father's partiality was obvious. Joseph was even given a beautiful coat of many colors, and he flaunted his father's favor in front of his brothers. He was a talebearer, running back to Jacob with reports about the other sons. He also earned their enmity by telling about dreams he had, which he interpreted to mean that the other brothers, and even his father and mother, would bow down to him. The likelihood of such a thing happening seemed remote, but still the brothers *hated him yet more for his dreams and for his words.* (Gen. 37:8)

Feelings ran so high that while he was still a teenager, Joseph was taken by his brothers and sold into slavery. (Even his beautiful coat was taken away, soaked with blood, and returned to his father, who believed his son dead.)

From being the pampered favorite of a rich patriarch, Joseph became a slave. He was taken to Egypt by Midianite traders, and there he was sold to Potiphar, the captain of the pharaoh's guard. Certainly it would seem that his fortunes had been reversed. But not for long!

Joseph might have lost his freedom, but he had by no means given up his belief in God as his supply. In the household of the Egyptian *the Lord was with Joseph, and he became a successful man.* (Gen. 39:2)

As a matter of fact, his master was so impressed with Joseph's ability to attract prosperity that pretty soon he appointed him overseer over all his wealth. Potiphar trusted Joseph so completely that he *had no concern for anything but the food which he ate.* (Gen. 39:6) Things were going well for Joseph, but again hard times were ahead.

Joseph was falsely accused by Potiphar's wife and thrown into prison.

At this point Joseph had plenty of excuses for failure, lack, and limitation. But he was not a person to make excuses. Again he set to work to make the best of his situation. He so proved his abilities that before long the keeper of the prison singled him out and gave him more and more authority.

Finally, although Joseph was still a prisoner,

the keeper of the prison committed to Joseph's care all the prisoners who were in the prison; and whatever was done there, he was the doer of it; the keeper of the prison paid no heed to anything that was in Joseph's care, because the Lord was with him; and whatever he did, the Lord made it prosper. (Gen. 39:22, 23) Again, Joseph had gone as far as he could under the circumstances. He had made the most of the situation, but he did long to be free.

In the course of his duties, Joseph met two men who had been imprisoned, the pharaoh's butler and baker. Both had dreams, which Joseph interpreted for them. The butler would be returned to favor in three days, and the baker would be executed. It happened just as Joseph had said. Before the butler left Joseph requested: *"Remember me, when it is well with you, and do me the kindness, I pray you, to make mention of me to Pharaoh, and so get me out of this house."* (Gen. 40:14) But the chief butler went on his way and apparently forgot all about the Hebrew who had interpreted his dream.

Two years passed. Finally, Joseph's great opportunity came, and he was ready. When no one could interpret a dream which greatly troubled the pharaoh, the butler remembered the young Hebrew; and he was brought from the prison. Joseph explained to the king that there would be seven years of plenty followed by seven years of famine. The dream had been given so that provision could be made during the first seven years for the seven years of lack.

The pharaoh was so impressed with the young man that he told him: *"Since God has shown you all this, there is none so discreet and wise as you are; you shall be over my house, and all my people shall order themselves as you command; only as regards the throne will I be greater than you."* (Gen. 41:39)

At the age of thirty, after working his way through tremendous challenges, Joseph was the richest, most powerful executive in the rich and powerful land of Egypt, second only to the king.

Seven years later he was even more powerful. During the years of plenty, he had supervised the storing of great quantities of food against the day of famine, and when lack and limitation began to be felt in the land, he was the one who doled out the food.

As time passed, because of the pharaoh's dream and Joseph's stewardship, Egypt was the only land where food was available, and in the long run even the other sons of Jacob had to come to Egypt to buy grain. There they bowed down to Joseph as he had prophesied. And in time Jacob and all his retinue moved to Egypt, where Joseph provided for them. He not only prospered himself, but he caused a multitude of others to prosper as well.

What was Joseph's secret?

Joseph was a person who did not depend on outer circumstances for his prosperity. He looked to God, the Source within; and as he did, he prospered wherever he was. There are lessons here for us. We too can prosper under all circumstances.

When we learn to find the opportunities wherever we are and to look to the source of true prosperity within, we will find that we too can be rich and successful regardless of what others are doing and regardless of the circumstances in which we find ourselves at a given time.

First, let us consider some "don'ts," some mistakes that we must avoid if we are going to accept our riches from God.

Don't spend time and energy asking, "Why."

We may or may not be able to see just why certain experiences come into our lives. We may or may not understand basic causes in our daily affairs. We may or may not feel that we have brought certain difficulties on ourselves. But in the long run it behooves us to take constructive measures to remedy wrong conditions, not to bemoan our fate while asking, "Why did this happen to me?"

Under no circumstances should we waste time and effort in condemning ourselves for taking the wrong turn or even speaking out of turn. In the area of prosperous living there is no room for censure and disparagement, even when we are unhappy with our own actions. Instead, let us do what we can to correct the wrong and then get on with the business of building a life, as Joseph did.

If we can see what we have done to attract error conditions, then we can start to work to remedy wrong thoughts, correct conditions caused by wrong words, or make right decisions to counteract mistakes made in the past. This is a part of our constructive activity, reconstructing our lives in the light of our present understanding.

Suppose, though, we just can't see any reason why certain experiences have come to us. Then let's not spend time looking for someone to blame, and let's not spend hours soul-searching, looking for an answer to "Why?" Instead, let's adopt a constructive attitude that will bring the blessing forth wherever we are, just as Joseph did.

Did Joseph know what errors he had made, what he had done to attract hard conditions?

We have no way of knowing because he didn't waste time and energy being concerned with past mistakes. Instead, he made the most of the present moment in any situation in which he found himself.

Some of Joseph's faults were obvious, and they were character traits that had to be corrected before he was ready for the great assignment, carrying with it wealth and prestige that God had for him.

As a child, he was probably arrogant, recognizing that he was his father's favorite. He likely flaunted his position before the other brothers, and he was noted for carrying tales. Not only that, but he told the whole family about his dream in which they all bowed down to him. When his brothers sold him into slavery, it was undoubtedly the result of his attitude and actions toward them.

Did Joseph know what he had done wrong? It really doesn't matter, because in the long run he did correct those character faults. Whether he was aware of what he was doing is unimportant. But we can take a great lesson from Joseph.

Instead of moping around feeling sorry for himself, he got busy wherever he was, making the most of the situation. He didn't waste time asking, "Why?"

Don't resist or resent or plan revenge.

One sure way to delay your good is to devote your energies to anger and resistance, and you can't plan success while you are busy planning revenge.

As far as we know, Joseph didn't waste time or effort looking back. Certainly by the time his brothers came to Egypt to buy grain from him he had overcome any resentment he may have ever had against them. First, he tested them. Then he provided generously for his whole family during the remaining years of the famine.

When he came to Potiphar's house, Joseph had a choice. He could concentrate on anger and resentment and plot revenge, even if it was only in wishful thinking. Or he could get busy and prosper wherever he was. He chose the latter. And, had he wracked his brain, he could never have come up with a more fitting punishment for his brothers than he had when he revealed himself—the second most powerful man in Egypt—to them years later.

Again when he was put in prison, falsely accused, Joseph had to decide whether he would think of himself as abused or take hold of the situation and make the most of it. In order to prosper, he had to dedicate his thoughts and feelings to the positive approach only. And he did.

Do know that you are the ultimate master of your own soul.

It doesn't matter what happens to you. It doesn't matter what conditions surround you. It does matter greatly what happens through you. You are the only one who can pull you up or keep you down!

Each person possesses his or her own soul, but the person may allow himself or herself to be possessed by wrong ideas. That is the choice of the individual.

Joseph, who became a slave, was already so much in tune with God that he knew that no one could enslave his soul. Never in his mind was he a slave. Had he been, he would not have been qualified for the responsibilities he earned.

This young man maintained his dignity under all circumstances. He stood out so strongly as a person who was ready for authority that wherever he went, no matter what the circumstances, he ended up on top!

Others admired him and recognized his special qualities. The Egyptian captain was so impressed with his bearing and his apparent faith in God that he trusted him implicitly, turning over all his assets to this person of a different culture and religion.

Even slavery cannot bind the soul of one who

is expressing his own innate divinity.

Do visualize the good in every situation.

Even in what must have been his most difficult overcoming, Joseph was able to see the good. He had been sold into slavery by his own brothers. According to all appearances, he had no hope of ever seeing again those he loved. He was a foreigner in Egypt, and a slave at that! What good could he expect?

Yet years later, when his brothers feared Joseph's revenge, this great man clearly showed what he had been thinking when he stated: *"As for you, you meant evil against me; but God meant it for good."* (Gen. 50:20)

All through his life he found the blessing by expecting it, by imaging the good in his mind, by extracting every last bit of the good in every circumstance that came.

If we would experience prosperity, we too must learn to image in our minds the idea of plenty, even in the midst of lack. We must hold fast to the picture of opportunity, even where there appears to be none.

As we hold visual images of prosperity and success, we will find ways of bringing the good about, regardless of how conditions and people seem to hold us back. True wealth is everywhere waiting for us to call it out, no matter how well it may be hidden. We do this by seeing it in our minds so strongly that we won't settle for anything less. When the image is strong enough, the good must express.

Do give God the credit for your prosperity.

If we are to continue to enjoy true abundance, we must give God complete credit for our prosperity—not because God needs our credit or our words, but because we can only draw forth a continuing supply when we recognize the Source.

Everything originates in God. There is no other source in the universe. How ridiculous for someone to say, "I did it all by myself."

When we are truly wise and wealthy, we will continually give God His due. We will look to Spirit for our supply, and we will give thanks continually for the good in whatever form it comes.

One channel for Joseph's prosperity was his ability to interpret dreams. This clearly was a gift of God, and he made sure that this was understood. Even when he was standing for the first time before the powerful king of Egypt, he was careful to explain that he was simply God's channel. He said: *"It is not in me; God will give Pharaoh a favorable answer."* (Gen. 41:16)

Joseph's way to prosperity applies to any situation we can possibly find. His method of finding the blessing in every place will work for us today. We can be prosperous, no matter what the circumstances, when we refuse to waste time and energy on idle questioning and complaining, as well as resentment and anger, and give our full attention to taking mastery over ourselves, visualizing the good everywhere, and above all, giving credit to God.

We too can be rich and successful!

Remember: ... *whatever he did, the Lord made it prosper.*

How to Increase Production

We all want to produce more blessings in our lives! Each person has an innate desire to experience more of God's good, to make a lasting impression on the world, to sow and to reap the blessings of the universe. In order to do this, we must increase production—our own production. And each of us must do that for himself.

We can learn how to produce more on the job and prosper accordingly. We can acquire the skill to perform household tasks more quickly and easily and remove some of the burdens in our lives. In many ways we can become more efficient, success-oriented disciples in living and reap the rewards of prosperity, success, joy, and fulfillment that come from making the most of our powers and abilities.

Business and industries are constantly employing experts to study production methods and come up with better, quicker, easier ways of getting results. The premise is that a better way will result in greater volume, a quality product, more efficiency of operation, and consequently higher profits.

The principles that work for business and industry can be applied to improving our own life situation. We too can learn to accomplish more with greater ease, and we can improve the total quality of our lives. We can become more efficient in living, and we can increase our prosperity and the return of all good accordingly. Not only that, but we have our own internal expert to advise us on the changes we must make in order to increase our own production of good.

Consider the life of Jesus Christ as a model of efficiency.

What other person in history has affected so many lives so profoundly over such a long period of time? What other individual in three short years produced such a pronounced effect that 2,000 years later we are still seeking to understand just a fraction of the tremendous wisdom and insight He so freely shared with all?

Many of His instructions were designed to help us learn to live the more efficient life, but perhaps one of the least understood examples was given in the cursing of the barren fig tree.

Through the years, experts have disagreed on the meaning of this story of the fig tree. Some have felt it was not in keeping with Jesus' character to curse anything—certainly not a growing, living tree. Others have interpreted this to be some symbolic vindictiveness on Jesus' part—a condemnation of certain people, perhaps.

In Unity we understand that this story was not an expression of Jesus' personality on a human level, but it is another of the many wonderful lessons He so lovingly shared with us.

It was Monday morning of the week we now refer to as Holy Week. Jesus and the disciples had spent the night at Bethany and were walking to Jerusalem to spend the day.

As they walked, Jesus apparently was hungry, and He turned aside toward a fig tree near the road. But when He reached it, He could see that there was no fruit on the tree—just foliage.

On this particular type of tree, the fruit should appear before the leaves. Had the tree been productive, it would have contained figs along with the leaves. But it was barren. The tree was wasting itself in leaves and producing no figs, the figs or fruit being its reason for existence.

So Jesus gave another of His lessons by example. He cursed the barren fig tree, saying: *"May no fruit ever come from you again!"* (Matt. 21:19)

Immediately the tree withered away. While the disciples marveled at the shriveled fig tree, Jesus followed up with another lesson, this one on faith.

He taught: *"Truly, I say to you, if you have faith and never doubt, you will not only do what has been done to the fig tree, but even if you say to this mountain, 'Be taken up and cast into the sea,' it will be done. And whatever you ask in prayer, you will receive, if you have faith."* (Matt. 21:21, 22)

This is a two-fold message for all of us.

For the sake of our own well-being and spiritual growth, we must produce the fruits of our own higher nature for our nourishment and unfoldment. If we deny our innate nature and compromise with life in order to attain temporary results, we will sooner or later feel the results in decreased good (no figs or fruits).

Should this happen, we are not to curse ourselves, but we are to rid ourselves of the conditions, thoughts, and feelings that are keeping us from enjoying the full, rich, happy, successful life God intends us to have. If we would bring forth the fruit we desire, we must eliminate those concepts and emotions that are decreasing our productivity. If harvesttime is not producing an abundance of all good for us, then it behooves us to look to the inner life for barren fig trees. When we root them out and get rid of them, we will have room for right thoughts and feelings to grow and for the resultant right conditions to come forth.

The second lesson is also important. Here Jesus speaks once again of faith as the faculty that is unlimited in producing good results. With enough faith, we don't have to stop at the small fig trees in our thoughts and feelings. We can eventually even eliminate those mountains of long-standing error and deeply-rooted perversions of Truth. We can totally rearrange the contour of our lives to produce efficient, happy results.

We are just beginning to discover the tremendous blessings of good that God has in store for us, His children. But in order to claim them fully, in order to become the happy, fulfilled people we are supposed to be, we must counteract the bad habits of past thinking by shriveling the unproductive fig trees in our minds and by moving the mountains. Then there will be more room for the good to grow.

If you have wondered why some blessing you have sought seems to be delayed, why not appoint yourself the efficiency expert to increase your production of good thoughts only? Why not start to improve your life by eliminating wasted effort and destructive attitudes and emotions? These are your barren fig trees.

Here are some "dos" and "don'ts" that will enable you to free yourself from barren habits and produce good results in your life.

Don't look to others to provide your good.

Many people try to evade all responsibility for their own lives by looking to others to do for them what they are unwilling to do for themselves. They complain, "Why don't 'they' do something about it?" This serves as a good excuse for not taking action themselves. It's just one of the barren bushes that can take up time and thought without producing any good.

Others are so concerned with what the other fellow is or isn't doing that they completely ignore their own responsibilities and possibilities.

Consider the man who commented, "That's the laziest man I've ever seen. He's been sitting there for two hours doing nothing."

His friend asked, "How do you know?"

"Why, I've been watching him. That's how I know for sure!"

We can't produce figs or any other fruit by sitting around watching others, wondering why they aren't working. And when we see that our business is to follow our own inner Spirit of good to a more productive life, we will be happy to discard such habits.

Then there are people like the little girl in Sunday school.

Her teacher told the story of the Good Samaritan, and when she finished, she asked the class, "What does that lesson teach you?"

One child responded immediately, "That when I'm in trouble, someone should help me."

If we truly want to produce more good in our lives, we will not be concerned because others aren't jumping to help us, but we will seek out ways in which we can help others. Giving is one of the most effective methods of producing more blessings in our own lives, a way of attracting great returns. We can't afford the barren bush that spends time and energy looking for someone else to provide our good. When we eliminate that, we may see clearly just exactly what we can do to help ourselves; and from there it is just a short step to the fulfillment of our every need.

Don't hold on to old, unproductive thoughts.

The worker who truly desires to be efficient is constantly learning new ways of doing his job by eliminating wasted effort and streamlining the whole operation.

We can streamline our life's activity by eliminating all those old habits of thought and feeling that are interfering with our ability to do an effective job of living.

Our whole world's progress is the result of constantly replacing old concepts—even those good ones that may have served a constructive purpose at one time—with newer, better ways of doing things. If a better idea comes along, those who are contributing most to the forward movement of the human race will be willing to release the old to implement the new methods. It is simply a matter of progress.

So it is in our lives. Some concepts may have served well in the past. They may have been necessary to our position or consciousness at that time. But if they no longer produce good results for us, then it is time to release them for a higher goal.

On another occasion Jesus told a parable about a barren fig tree. The owner informed his gardener: "*'Lo, these three years I have come seeking fruit on this fig tree, and I find none. Cut it down; why should it use up the ground?'*" (Luke 13:7)

But the man who took care of the trees was reluctant. He begged: "*'Let it alone, sir, this year also, till I dig about it and put on manure.'*"

We too may be reluctant to give up something that is familiar—habits that have become a part of our human nature, even though we can see that they are not doing us any good. We, like the gardener, may plead, "Just let me keep it a little longer." But if we are to produce a continuing supply of blessings for ourselves and others, we must give up the lesser, often destructive concepts in order to employ the greater habits of mentally and spiritually claiming our good.

Don't perpetuate "time killers."

Wasted motion and wasted moments cut down production. Perhaps there are "time killers" in your life that you may not have recognized or that you may have felt powerless to change.

One of the most common types of "time killer" is the human relationship that has languished into a mutual effort to avoid productive activity.

A woman I know had a neighbor who was a very good friend but also a "time killer." Since she had no children and few responsibilities at home, she came over each morning after her husband left for work and settled down to drink coffee and chat for most of the day.

The first woman asked me, "What can I do without hurting her feelings? I can't get my work done."

She had to uproot the barren fig tree that was

making her frustrated and unproductive. So I suggested that she let the neighbor know she enjoyed her company but had some important work in the household that she simply had to do. Pretty soon the neighbor became so bored with her friend's housekeeping that she decided to take a part-time job.

In the long run, both women were much happier and more productive, and they remained good friends. Sometimes we have to take a stand for what is right and necessary.

We all need times of rest and relaxation and fulfilling social contacts, but "time killers" have no place in an interesting, productive life. By putting God first and letting Him guide us in our human relationships, we will eliminate those insidious interrupters of our progress in living.

And if we need help in taking the necessary step, we will find that God within us is equal to the task.

Sometimes we may confuse our responsibilities toward other people with "time killers" and justify wasting our time and energy trying to meet all the demands of others.

Should this happen to you, remember that Jesus fulfilled His responsibilities perfectly and beautifully. Even from the Cross, He, as the eldest son, placed His mother in the care of

John, the beloved disciple.

But on another occasion, when He was speaking to a group, He was interrupted with the news that His mother and brothers wanted to see Him. Discerning immediately which activity was more important, He replied: *"Who is my mother, and who are my brothers? . . . whoever does the will of my Father in heaven is my brother, and sister, and mother."* (Matt. 12:48, 50)

Jesus had a set of values based on a firm commitment to God; and because of this, He not only was able to make the right choice at any given time, but He also was able to act without wondering, "What will people say?" Guided by the Spirit of God within Him, He fulfilled His responsibilities, but He refused to stop His ministry for "time killers."

When we turn to God first, we too will make right choices while fulfilling those obligations that are really important.

Do give your best where you are.

Some people feel that they will reserve their best efforts for sometime in the future, when it will be more worthwhile.

There is only one place we can learn to live effectively and efficiently, and that is where we are. When we put off our concentrated attempt to do a good job until sometime when we feel the situation merits it, we will find that things just don't improve enough for us to ever give life our best. (And when we don't give our best to life, we may be sure that we will not receive the best in return. The law of giving and receiving always works.)

Wherever we are, we serve a purpose, and there is something there that we can do better than any other person. If we want to reap the rewards, we must learn to concentrate on giving our best effort right here, now. We must bring forth fruit in our present situation. When we do, we will grow into the more productive experiences of life. And not only that, we will be prepared to handle the better position, the higher income, the greater responsibility when they come.

Do trust God to help you.

You are God's beloved child, and the good He has for you is above and beyond anything you can even contemplate in your human thinking at this time. Faith is the key that unlocks the door to the good He has prepared.

We must learn to go forward doing the best we can and trusting God to do the rest. When we give our lives absolutely into His care and keeping, while continuing to produce the fruit as best we can, He takes over in ways that may seem mysterious to one in human consciousness. But they work! They bring forth the harvest of good.

Building faith that gets results may take time, or it may be so strong in a certain situation that the answer we seek is immediate. But faith in God will increase production—through us and to us.

Once, when I was lecturing in another city, a man in the audience came to me afterward and wanted to share his story.

He said that a few years earlier he had been "a real drunkard in this town." He spent so much time under the influence of alcohol that his productivity was nil and his life was totally meaningless.

On one occasion he had been drinking for a week and knew he had simply reached the end of his rope. The only apparent way out for him at that point was to commit suicide. So he sent his wife and son away from home and started trying to figure out how to go about killing himself.

He never was sure exactly how it happened, but suddenly he had the urge to talk to God, to whom he had had nothing to say for years. The words flowed through his mind, almost unbidden.

He found himself declaring, "God, there's nothing I can do. You take over." Then he fell across the bed and went to sleep. When he awakened, he had no desire for a drink, and he never drank alcohol again. For him the need and the trust and release were so great that the healing came forth quickly; and because it was what he truly desired, it lasted!

We can increase productivity in any area of our lives by simply turning to God in trust, knowing that, as we do our part, He will do the rest.

We are designed to bring forth wonderful blessings in God's universe. We are to produce good for our own enjoyment, and we are to share it with others. When we get rid of the "time killers" and other unproductive thoughts and feelings and begin to give our best to life where we are, we can know without a doubt that God will prosper us. We can trust Him utterly to use us to produce His good in His world!

How to Cure Hurt Feelings

Two friends built homes on adjoining acreage. They had great plans for the area, including an airport that would be for a joint investment.

Soon after they moved in, one man asked the other, "Would you mind if I cut down a few trees on your property? It would certainly improve my view."

The neighbor adamantly refused to let the friend touch even one tree on his land, and the first man became offended—not only offended, but badly hurt by the refusal. So he retaliated.

A source of great pride with the second neighbor was the frog pond that occupied space on both parcels of land. The man whose feelings had been hurt went out and drained his half of the pond, which happened to be the lower end. Naturally, that was the end of the frog pond; and the other man felt he had to retaliate.

This true story of two men who started out as friends and neighbors deteriorated into a continuing battle of hurt feelings, each man trying to outdo the other in arranging unpleasant surprises for the other. And so it went as long as they lived on the adjoining properties where they had started out with such high hopes.

What they didn't understand is that no one can afford hurt feelings. No one can harbor the corrosive emotion of feeling oppressed or persecuted without harming himself or herself mentally, emotionally, physically, and in the area of human relationships.

Retaliation doesn't solve the problem, either. It simply aggravates the situation. It is a law of the universe that you cannot hurt another without also hurting yourself.

So what can you do when someone does something that seems to be a breach of friendship or a betrayal of trust? How can you cure hurt feelings?

From time to time, Jesus had to deal with hurt feelings among the disciples, as each one wanted to be first. It seemed easy for them to become competitive and offended at small things.

On several occasions the disciples squabbled

among themselves trying to determine who would be the greatest in Jesus' kingdom. Jesus refused to recognize the possibility of hurt feelings and reminded them to be teachable and trusting, as little children, and not assertive and contentious.

Even at the Last Supper, a time that was very important in Jesus' life, those who were closest to Him were arguing among themselves. He was trying to share His deep feelings with them and they were concerned about who was going to be most important. But Jesus did not become offended at their callous lack of concern. Even when the disciples fell asleep in the Garden of Gethsemane, after He had asked them to keep watch with Him, He was understanding and forgiving. He didn't believe in hurt feelings, and He continued to demonstrate individual freedom and authority. At the same time, He showed proper concern for others. While the disciples argued among themselves in the upper room, He picked up a towel and took over a servant's job, washing their feet to show the value of service.

With the intuitive knowing that characterized His relationships with others, Jesus perceived in advance that Peter would betray Him three times before the Crucifixion. Even this didn't make Him bitter. And He was careful to give Peter the opportunity to make amends (once for each betrayal) when He appeared to the disciples after the Resurrection.

Three times Jesus asked Peter: " . . . *do you love me?"* (John 21:17) The disciple, not understanding the Master's way, was grieved because Jesus asked the question more than once. After he had assured Jesus of his love, Jesus gave him specific instruction: *"Feed my sheep."* (John 21:17) Peter's job had been assigned.

But Peter wasn't willing to just go ahead and do the work. He looked around and saw John, and immediately he began to think in terms of competition and hurt feelings. He asked: *"Lord, what about this man?"* (John 21:21) Jesus answered with another question: *"If it is my will that he remain until I come, what is that to you? Follow me!"* (John 21:22)

A tremendous teaching! When we are following the Christ, we do not have time for hurt feelings or undue concern about what another is doing. Jesus says to each of us, "What is that to you? Why are you wasting time and effort on what the other person is doing? Follow the Christ, the Spirit of God within you!"

There are two basic causes of hurt feelings.

First, when you let yourself be disturbed and upset because of something another has done, you are making the decision to let that other person control what goes on inside you.

Actually, no other person can hurt your feelings or upset your peace of mind. No one can climb inside your soul and make you react in a certain way. All another can do is to provide a stimulus. You determine how you are going to react to it. If you decide to become upset about a certain incident and to harbor feelings of distress and injury, that is a decision you make for yourself.

Jesus provided a way out that applies to any situation in which you feel hurt or upset. Ask yourself, "What is that to me? I have a Spirit within me that is greater than anything anyone can do or say. I am the Christ." Claim it. Declare it. Live with it. Concentrate on it so strongly that all thought and even memory of the offense fade away.

But suppose someone does something that seemingly injures you, mentally or physically. Do you simply let him perpetuate the wrong? No, of course not. You use wisdom in all your dealings with others. But by following the guidance of the Christ within, God's own Spirit in you, you do whatever needs to be done—without any human sense of retaliation, but rather with peace and freedom in your own self.

There is always a right way to handle any

situation. But there is only One who can reveal it to you, the Spirit of God in the depths of your being, the One who speaks in such a small voice that you can't hear it unless you are willing to become still and listen.

The second cause of hurt feelings can perhaps best be illustrated by the children's game of "follow the leader." The challenge is to do whatever the leader does, no matter how silly or dangerous.

Sometimes people carry this idea of patterning their lives on the expected actions and reactions into their adult activity. They look to see what others are doing and then act accordingly. They are so busy watching the other fellow that they may not really have time to build lives of their own.

If another person gets a promotion on the job, they fall into the trap of feeling hurt and resentful because the opportunity didn't come to them. After all, they argue, it is "natural" to feel hurt.

They are still playing the game. They are giving the expected response of the human consciousness. They stay in the old rut because they are unwilling to learn a new way of living. And so they go through life fighting the world and nursing hurt feelings.

Jesus gave us the answer. We do not have to

follow a human leader. We do not have to be one of the world's many sheep, influenced by first one person and then another, never making independent decisions.

There is only One who is qualified to be our Leader, and that is the Christ within us. When we are willing to follow the Spirit within us, we will not have difficulty making decisions. We will know what to do and we will do it. And if another receives a promotion we had expected, we will not become hurt. Rather, we will ask, "What is that to me? I bless him on his way. God is in charge of my life, and my own good comes to me in His right and perfect way."

Here are some "dos" and "don'ts" for learning to program our lives from within, thus curing all feelings that we have been maltreated or injured in some way.

Don't depend on others to build your self-image.

Many people are so concerned with the impression they are making on others that they literally come to see themselves as they think others see them.

Before making a move, they ask themselves, "What will people think?" And when others do not express approval and approbation, they withdraw into themselves to nurse their hurts and wonder what to try next to make others think well of them. Meanwhile, they find it impossible to build a strong self-image, because they are totally dependent on the approval of others.

We cannot afford to look to anyone or anything outside of ourselves for our self-esteem! We have to learn to establish an inner vision of self-worth, based on knowing ourselves as children of God, divinely endowed with all spiritual qualities. When we feel good within, we can then establish healthy relationships with others.

How do you think about yourself? Do you try to fulfill the expectations of others, wanting their approval, or are you willing to follow the way that is right for you?

In a visit to a nursing home, I became acquainted with a lively little lady who was always busy crocheting some item to give as a gift. She always seemed happy and interested.

Her roommate complained because she wouldn't join the group on the patio; but the lady with the crocheting told us, "I know they call me Princess and think I'm stuck-up. But I just don't like to listen to all of their gossip." What the others thought or said didn't bother her. She was too busy doing the thing that felt right and good to her. And she was happy with herself and others!

Don't expect appreciation.

What a happy surprise it can be to have someone say, "Thank you," for a gift or favor you have forgotten! What a disappointment it can be to wait for the appreciation that never comes.

Why do you give to others or do something nice for them? Is it for the return? Or is it because it is God's nature to give, and you are expressing His nature in you?

Many hurt feelings result from doing something for another in the expectation of return of gratitude. When the appreciation isn't forthcoming, the tendency is to be hurt, to cry, "Nobody cares. Nobody appreciates anything I do." (One incident is easily multiplied to encompass everybody and everything.)

If we are living in an attitude of healthy adjustment to ourselves and others, we will be giving. We will not give unwisely, as in the case of overindulgence of a child already spoiled. Neither will we continue to give to people who are unwilling to help themselves. But we will give joyously, freely, as God directs, without thought of return. With no expectation of thanks, we won't be frustrated when it doesn't come. Instead, we will be happy and busy, and the appreciation (if it comes) will be just one of the bonuses of good along our way, not a cause of extreme elation or disappointment, but just a nice happening in our day.

Don't let the hurts build up.

It is always good to clear up negative feelings when they occur. Otherwise, they may attract others of their type and build a strong bulwark of distress and injury that is hard to penetrate. Small hurts may be handled easily if recognized and rejected at the time, but large injuries are reinforced by so many memories and so many strong emotions that removing them can be a monumental task. It can be done, but how much easier it is to take care of the little things as they arise!

Marriage counsellors particularly are aware of the danger of a build-up of hurt feelings. How often one partner becomes defensive about conditions and situations that exist only in mind—a fabrication of hurt feelings and frustrations. Allowing a series of incidents to pile up into a mountain of seemingly insurmountable problems can result in a broken marriage. But it doesn't have to happen! Understanding and communication will dissolve hurt feelings when they arise. And how much better it is to get rid of them when they are small.

Remember, all of us make ourselves miserable or happy by what we choose to think and feel. No one can make us happy, and no one has power to cause us to be unhappy. We choose, and when we begin rejecting little feelings of offense and injustice when they arise, when we handle situations with maturity and good judgment, then we will not allow a buildup of hurts in the first place.

Do "shake off the dust."

Jesus, recognizing the vulnerability of the disciples He sent out into the world to do missionary work, gave them specific instructions for avoiding hurt feelings. He sent out the twelve who were closest to Him, and He sent out seventy others later. In both cases He gave the same instructions. Knowing that they could only succeed in the work He had given them to do if they maintained their inner peace, He told them exactly how to react to the people they met.

First, they were to seek out individuals who might be receptive to their message and to their spiritual help. When they approached a home, they were to give the customary saluation to whoever opened the door. They were to speak the blessing, "Peace be to this house!" This was a way of establishing the right thoughts and feelings on both sides for a friendly, happy, and productive relationship.

But Jesus recognized the possibility that they

would be rejected in some quarters. So He made provision for that by adding: *"And if a son of peace is there, your peace shall rest upon him; but if not, it shall return to you."* (Luke 10:6) The Hebrew tradition was that a blessing refused would return to the sender, and Jesus was reminding the disciples of this. If someone refused to accept their peace, they should not become disturbed or upset. Rather, they should accept the peace as returned to them. In other words, they couldn't afford hurt feelings!

Then He gave them further instruction. The Master told them: *"And if any one will not receive you or listen to your words, shake off the dust from your feet as you leave that house or town."* (Matt. 10:14) This meant that they should deny the seeming reality of the whole situation and simply release it into nothingness. If they refused to carry it with them in thought, it would have no power over them. It would not be able to hurt or harm them in any way.

We too can follow Jesus' way by letting our peace return to us if it is rejected by others, by refusing to let ourselves become upset or disturbed, regardless of what the others do. And when we reach the point of shaking off the dust, we can so completely release the whole situation that we forget it ever happened. Then there is not even one iota of a seed for hurt feelings! It is gone for good.

The men who were sent out by Jesus to do spiritual work could not afford the luxury of hurt feelings. And neither can we allow such emotions to interfere with our ability to function in an orderly, effectual way.

Do follow the Christ within.

Instead of following the crowd, instead of reacting in a human way, we can learn in all situations to turn first to the Spirit of God within us. When we are following the Christ, as Jesus instructed Peter to do, we are on our way to right answers and joyous, freeing feelings. We will live in a God-centered world and will work with a God-centered attitude that doesn't waste time and effort on nonproductive thoughts and emotions.

When Jesus said to Peter: *"Follow me!"* (John 21:19) He was speaking not just to one disciple, but to all who want to learn His way, to do His work, and to feed His sheep. When we direct ourselves to spiritual purposes, we will not have the time or inclination to deal in petty incidents or human bickering. We will walk in the serenity of our own inner peace, based on knowing ourselves as children of God and His own appointed peacemakers. We will not look to other people for approval and status as human beings, but we will seek always to satisfy the demands of our own spiritual nature, that part of us that is above all human limitations.

We will be loving, kind, and thoughtful—not because others are loving, kind, and thoughtful, but because we are following the Christ way of life and growth.

We will have a healthy feeling about ourselves—not because we are on an "ego trip," but because we believe in our spiritual nature, our own divine potentiality, and we know that the best way to express our higher nature is to claim it now.

Following the Christ is a life-long project in itself, and it will bring tremendous benefits in the long run. Curing hurt feelings is just one small bonus along the way of knowing ourselves as God's channels, necessary for His work on Earth. But when we no longer spend time and energy nursing negative reactions to the happenings in our lives, think how much more we have to give to the large spiritual purposes for which we are destined!

Hurt feelings confine us to a small world of human action and interaction. Following the Christ widens our horizons to a very large, God-centered world, where first things come first and progress is continuous.

As children of God, it is our business to

"shake off the dust" and get on with the business of being what we are designed to be — happy, healthy, productive, and at peace.

How to Get More Out of Life

Are you getting all you want out of life? Is each day a rich, happy experience of living and growing? Do you welcome even the challenges and trials as times of productive activity, times of overcoming?

Americans live in the richest country in recorded history, and people in many other countries enjoy a high standard of living. Even most so-called poor persons have wealth above and beyond that of just a few years ago. Then why isn't everyone happy? Why aren't we all radiant and free, joyous and enthusiastic, filled with happy expectation all the time? Why don't we greet each day with a smile and sing our way through it? How can we learn to awaken more life in our everyday activity of living?

The Bible has an answer for us. In the Book of Revelation, the glorified Being who spoke to John gave him messages for the angels of seven churches. These churches stand for states of consciousness, ways of thinking and feeling in us, and the messages give us clues for changing ourselves and improving our life-styles.

One of the messages was for the angel of the church at Laodicea, a city in Asia Minor, about forty miles from Ephesus. The Speaker first described the Laodicean way of thinking then gave the remedy for it.

These people were completely enmeshed in the material and intellectual parts of life and living. They found their satisfaction in the possession of things, the admiration of their friends, and the positions they occupied in life. They were so preoccupied with accumulating wealth and fitting into the status quo that they completely immersed themselves in their day-to-day lives. Had someone suggested that they lacked some important part of life, they would have pointed to their material wealth, position, and power as signs that they lacked nothing.

The writer of Revelation describes them this way:

" 'I know your works: you are neither cold nor hot. Would that you were cold or hot! So, because you are lukewarm, and neither cold nor hot, I will spew you out of my mouth. For you say, I am rich, I have prospered, and I need nothing; not knowing that you are wretched, *pitiable, poor, blind, and naked.' "* (Rev. 3:15-17)

This is a description that fits many people today—those who go through life enmeshed in the material side of their nature, feeling themselves rich because they have the wealth of the world at hand. They claim loudly that they are rich and successful, but inside they know that something is missing. There is simply no real and lasting satisfaction in a life that is all wrapped up in day-to-day living by the world's standards.

Even the person who feels most wealthy and successful in a material way will some day find himself eclipsed by a greater personality. And the mill wheel that grinds the material grain for the world wears thin and results in a monotony that can be only lukewarm at its best. This is the sort of person who may one day ask himself, "Is it all worthwhile, anyway?"

Joy and enthusiasm are the ingredients of a rich, happy, successful life; and monotony and boredom, the results of preoccupation with the world's demands and aims, cannot bring either. Existence in a materialistic rut of daily experience can only be brightened occasionally by momentary achievements that quickly pall.

Then what is the answer? How can we live a life that is meaningful and satisfying? Must we leave the world, with all its ruts of complacency, conformity, and continuity? Are we to get away from it all and simply start a new life-style?

Not necessarily. Many times the act of beginning a new life-style in some other place soon disintegrates into a new form of lukewarm living. If it simply represents a change in place and occupation, it doesn't bring about a real transformation at all.

But there is an answer. That answer may require that we seek another place, or it may not. It may mean that we will change occupations, or it may not. One thing we can be sure of—it will change us inside; and when that happens, we will light the fire of joy and enthusiasm, and whatever we do in outer ways will glow with warmth and love. There will be no more lukewarm living. We will be giving much to life from the rich store within us, and we will receive rich rewards in inner joy and satisfaction as well as the outer wealth that is not an end in itself but simply a bonus that accompanies our daily life experience. We will be getting much more out of life!

In effect, we are to learn to live by the rule that Jesus gave: *"Therefore do not be anxious, saying, 'What shall we eat?' or 'What shall we drink?' or 'What shall we wear?' For the Gentiles seek all these things; and your heavenly Father knows that you need them all. But seek first His kingdom and His righteousness, and all these things shall be yours as well."* (Matt. 6:31-33)

Rich living begins in us. Truly meaningful daily experiences are the result of our investment in life, our investment of ourselves in meaningful experiences of inner growth. We can never be truly happy if we are only lukewarm in our relationship to life. We can never experience the true riches of joyous attitudes when we limit ourselves to the material side alone. Life is much more than food and clothing, as Jesus said, and we must learn to put all things in their proper perspective if we are to enjoy everything life has to give us. We cannot do this if we are complacent and satisfied, judging ourselves by the world's standards. But we must learn to apply a new set of standards, one that will take us out of our ruts and give us a whole new view of the world and of ourselves as a part of it.

Now let us consider some "dos" and "don'ts" for learning to live richly, productively, and with depth and meaning for our lives. There is more to life than we have yet experienced. There is always more, because life is growth.

Don't ever be satisfied with things as they are.

Most people, when they think of being dissatisfied, come up with "wants" for a variety of material things — a new car, a new dress, a new home, and so on. This is not the type of dissatisfaction we are discussing here. We are talking about divine discontent.

Comparison of position and material assets with those of others may bring a feeling of superiority and condescension, or it may bring a feeling of envy or greed. Neither is healthy. The kind of dissatisfaction that leads to growth and to richer experiences in living is the feeling in us that there must be more to our everyday experiences — there must be something that will give life the depth and meaning that seem to be missing. (Even those who are seeking to improve their lives according to spiritual principles sometimes fall into the trap of comparing their lives with others and thinking of themselves as superior in some way.)

Divine discontent has nothing to do with making comparisons. As a matter of fact, it doesn't concern other people at all. It is something going on inside us. It is God speaking in the depths of our being, inviting, "Come up higher."

Life is growth, and if we are not growing, we will always have a feeling that something is missing. Whether we recognize it or cover it over with hurry and "busyness," it is there; and the inner voice will keep trying to get through until we stop ourselves and take time to listen, time to revamp and recoup our lives and choose a conscious direction toward the growth and joy and livingness our souls are seeking.

God needs us to express through. We are His hands and feet; and He will continue to knock at the door, to keep trying to get our attention, until eventually we do turn away from material pursuits alone and deepen and enrich our lives from within.

Don't just drift.

The majority of the people in our world today have not taken charge of their lives. They are doing the things that are expected of them, earning a living in a convenient niche, making money and spending it, and, in many cases, simply complaining their way through one boring day after another. They are drifting through life feeling that there should be more, but not knowing why something seems to be missing.

We all need aims and goals. We need to be living, not just existing through colorless experiences. It is important that we have a sense of purpose and direction. Without it, our lives would be monotonous and meaningless.

There is something else that we must understand. If we are not consciously taking charge of our own lives, someone else is.

Do we buy a certain brand of toothpaste because the attractive actress says she uses that kind? Do we install a particular type of burglar alarm because we are warned about dire consequences if we don't? Do we choose our clothes, deodorants, and soft drinks in the hope that they will somehow make us as popular and as happy as those people in the TV commercials appear to be?

Influencing others is one of the biggest businesses in the country today. Advertisements of all kinds urge various activities and purchases. Sales people push their products. Even those who would sell others on thinking their way on local, state, or national issues study the market to see how best to influence the greatest number of people. We are continually surrounded and bombarded by others' attempts to run our lives. (Most of them are professionals at the job.) If we are not careful, they may succeed in doing it. Those who are trying to influence us run the gamut from our closest friends to the biggest business. And if we are drifting, purposeless and bored, they will find a ready target.

The only way we can learn to live productive, happy, and useful lives is to take charge of them ourselves, to build our goals and aims on true and lasting values, and to live day by day with dedication and devotion, making the most of each moment and looking forward to the joy of the next.

The instructions to the Laodiceans give us some rules for taking charge of our lives, breaking out of the meaningless role of drifting and living by others' standards, and setting ourselves on fire with the joy that is ours when we start to claim our divine inheritance.

Do "buy . . . gold . . . and white garments . . . and salve." (Rev. 3:18)

The first thing we must do to awaken to rich living is to revise our set of values. No longer do we look to material things for our satisfaction. No longer can we be complacent and stationary.

The Laodiceans were instructed to break out of their lukewarm arrogance in this way:

"Buy from me gold refined by fire, that you may be rich, and white garments to clothe you and to keep the shame of your nakedness from being seen, and salve to anoint your eyes, that you may see." (Rev. 3:18)

The word "buy" refers to investing our inner resources, and the succeeding words tell us how to invest them.

Gold symbolizes the riches of Spirit. Instead of allowing our minds to be monopolized by the pressures of everyday living, we must charge them with rich spiritual concepts of life, love, joy, peace, wisdom, and freedom. These concepts are to be "refined in the fire" in the sense that they are to be taken out of the concept of material thinking and purified by spiritual motives and interests. We buy this gold by charging our minds with rich, true ideas of Spirit; and when we do, we are rich in mind and manifestation.

We are also to acquire white garments. White apparel always symbolizes purity of life and motive. When we buy this type of raiment, we clothe ourselves in pure thoughts and reject all limiting concepts and release all negative thinking and false standards. We literally surround ourselves with a thought aura of goodness and light. In this aura, we are guided and protected.

The "salve" that is our third purchase is perhaps the most difficult of all. This requires that we learn to look past appearances and see our world with a whole new viewpoint, with spiritual insight. Had we always held to the picture of ourselves and our world as the expression of God ideas, it would be easy to buy this eye salve. We would automatically look past appearances to the Truth. We would know ourselves as whole and perfect children of God, even in the midst of the evidence of disease and discord. We would look past limitations in such a way that we would always be expectant of greater opportunities and more reasons for enthusiasm and joy, regardless of what our circumstances seemed to be.

But the eye salve is something we must buy with the careful, conscientious watching of our thoughts. It can be ours only if we are willing to invest our time, attention, and energy in developing new habits of thinking, feeling, acting, and reacting—in other words, if we are willing to pay the price.

Do open the door.

The door of our hearts opens from within, and only we can open it. Yet always there is the knocking, the feeling that there is more to life and that we can be greater, happier, healthier, and freer.

Revelation puts it this way:

"Behold, I stand at the door and knock; if any one hears my voice and opens the door, I will come in to him and eat with him, and he with me." (Rev. 3:20) Quite an adventure in itself! However we imagine this visit with the Christ, it has to be especially meaningful and important to us.

But how do we answer the knock? How do we open the door? We do it by spending much time and thought on being receptive to God, learning to know His way and experiencing His presence and His power. We open the door through prayer, a spiritual process that goes on within us in a very special and personal way.

Only we can seek the Spirit of Truth within our own being. No other person can enter there. Another may point the way. Our own urge to be more and do more can inspire us to seek. But it is in the quiet place within ourselves, when we are cut off from all commotion and "busyness," when we are concentrating on God as He is in us as our own higher nature, that we are able to open the door to the Christ.

The rewards are great. When we have found this secret place within ourselves and invited the Christ into our lives, we eat of the rich ideas of substance and awaken ourselves to a new dimension in living. There is nothing on the human plane to equal this triumphant experience. There is nothing in the world that can give such true depth and meaning to life. It has to happen in us. And it does, when we open the door of our hearts, when we seek the spiritual answer with the certain knowledge that we will surely find it.

Do *"be zealous."*

Zeal is one of the little understood attributes of mind. Many people think of zeal as excitement, a busy running from one thing to another, or trying to excite and influence others.

Zeal, as with any of our twelve powers, may be directed to outer means. But when it is, it will deplete and even destroy. In its spiritual interpretation, zeal is not noisy but quiet. It is not a rushing but a glow, not a disturbance but a fire that makes each day meaningful and beautiful, and enthusiasm that means that life is truly worthwhile.

In the letter to the angel of the Laodiceans, we are told: "... *be zealous and repent.*" (Rev. 3:19) So the true expression of spiritual zeal comes about as the result of completely turning away from the old way of living, leaving behind the materialistic goals, and choosing new aims of spiritual growth and satisfaction. This doesn't take anything away from life but gives depth and meaning to even the most trivial everyday experience. When we work with God, we have a whole new set of values, and we have the enthusiasm to match.

We are still in the world. We may be doing the same sort of thing we have done for years. But, when we are on fire with God ideas, when we are completely alive, alert, and awake to our spiritual potential, then we are in a whole new realm. Everything takes on a radiance that comes from within us. Life is happy and fulfilling. It is adventurous. We go from day to day with expectation—no more "lukewarm" living. We awaken with enthusiasm for the opportunities in each new day. We live, instead of just existing, through a succession of rich, satisfying experiences.

This is the way we can claim every day the blessings of rich living that God has promised to all His children.

How to Recoup Your Losses

At one time or another, every person experiences a feeling of loss. This may come about because of the loss of a prized friendship, or perhaps the theft of some material treasure. It may be the result of a loss of job or of health or of money. Perhaps one experiences lost time as a failure and a waste.

Whether it is a matter of the misplacing of some much-needed cash or the overwhelming sense of bereavement that results from the passing of a loved one, the experience of loss can be traumatic. But under no circumstances should it be allowed to govern the rest of our lives.

Many people, concentrating on some deprivation in their lives, allow it to dominate their thinking over a period of years and actually keep them from living either profitably or pleasurably.

In spite of the shock that may come with some specific type of loss in our lives, we can recover our equilibrium and end up richer, happier, and healthier than we have ever been. We can, if we are willing to stop believing in the loss and start believing in ourselves and our future. Nothing is permanent. No loss is lasting. It remains a loss only as long as we hold it with the thought of deprivation in our minds.

In fact, many seeming losses hold the seed of greater blessings than we have ever known, when we are willing to release the old in order to lay hold of the greater good that is waiting. The lost job may impel us to seek the better one God has for us. The misplaced article may be found, while teaching us a much-needed lesson of conservation. The healing need may alert us to thoughts that need to be corrected in mind, or it may provide time for spiritual contemplation. When we get rid of the thought of the loss, very often we find that nothing has been lost after all, and we reap a rich blessing from the whole experience.

The prophet Joel had to deal with the idea of loss when he started his ministry to the Jewish people. It was during the Persian rule over Judea, and the Jews had suffered greatly because of the destruction of their crops by locusts.

Joel felt that the problem was indicative of the fact that the people had gone away from God in their thinking, and he advocated a return to spiritual thinking and activity.

Never at any time did he indicate in any way that he felt the problem was hopeless. He recognized that there had been a challenge, but he also was quick to point out that it was not necessary to stay in the thought of lack. Not only that, but the limitation of the past could be filled so completely that the people would have more than ever. (This, of course, is also the theme of the book of Job, which was written during the same time period.)

Joel spoke God's promise which has brought heart to many over the years:

"I will restore to you the years which the swarming locust has eaten . . . You shall eat in plenty and be satisfied, and praise the name of the Lord your God, who has dealt wondrously with you." (Joel 2:25, 26)

Not only can we have restoration of our seemingly lost good, but we can have a greater blessing that will erase even the memory of those years. The good can flow in such abundance into our lives that we will forget all misery and unhappiness of the past. It is a beautiful promise!

Of course, this promise applies specifically

to our present moment. God can fill it so full of love and joy and peace and blessings of mind and matter that nothing in the past matters at all. And gradually, it fades away, until even the memory vanishes. If we think of the loss at all, it is as though it happened to someone else and doesn't concern the happy, fulfilled, rich person we have become.

Those years lost to the locusts represent any periods of our lives that seem to be devoid of good. And the locusts to which they are given are the swarming thoughts that fill our minds with concepts of lack and limitation, mistreatment and misery, hopelessness and fear. Always the continuation of negation and lack is an expression of something we hold in mind. People, things, and situations come to play a particular part in our lives and then pass out of them. It is our own sense of loss that perpetuates the tragedy instead of the blessing.

Joel was quite clear in telling the Jewish people that what was needed was a change of mind. He didn't offer to pray that God would replace the lost crops without any effort on their part. Instead, he pointed to the importance of transforming their thoughts. He instructed:

"...rend your hearts and not your garments." Return to the Lord, your God, for he *is gracious and merciful* . . .   (Joel 2:13)

It didn't matter whether they went into elaborate outer ceremonies, such as tearing their garments. But their repentance should be a change of thought, a transformation of consciousness, a return to spiritual awareness. When this was done, the loss would be quickly forgotten in the joy of new and greater abundance.

And so it is with us. We cannot only forget our losses, not only recoup what appeared to be gone, but we can be richer, happier, healthier than ever when we release all thought of lack in our minds and return to God's abundance in our every thought and feeling.

If we have held very long and very strongly to the feeling that we have been deprived of some good, it may take time and energy to transform the thought patterns in our minds. But it can be done; and when it is, even those years that were lost to the locusts will become as nothing, because we will be so enthusiastic about life and interested in the blessings of the present.

At the time of an experience in which something precious seems to be moving out of our lives, we may feel that the way is dark and the future is hopeless. But when we break out into the light of God's morning, we see that there is a blessing in everything, and nothing has the power to take from us our joy and our faith in living.

Now let us consider some "dos" and "don'ts" for recouping any losses we may have endured.

Don't concentrate on loss.

When we concentrate, we center all our attention on a particular thought and the emotions that support it. That is fine, when it is something we want to perpetuate and increase. But when it is a negative condition, such as loss, we must learn to withdraw our attention and our strong support from the whole concept. We cannot afford to continue to think in terms of loss!

A good statement for retraining our minds is one that Unity students have used for years: *Nothing is lost in Spirit.* More than one lost item has been located when the individual began remembering that, in Spirit, nothing is ever missing. Inasmuch as we are one with God Mind, everything we need to know is easily available to us. Sometimes simply repeating the words *nothing is lost in Spirit* will bring an idea that will instantly lead one to the misplaced item.

The statement is also good in dealing with other experiences of loss.

Suppose you have become depressed because of the passing of a loved one. At such a time it is human to experience an overwhelming sense of loss and a feeling that a great void has been made in your life, perhaps one that can never be filled. Even then remind yourself that, in Spirit, nothing can ever be lost. Perhaps you no longer have the daily presence of a loved one on this plane, but think of the blessings you have shared in the past! No one can ever take them from you. Of course, you may become so busy being sorry for yourself that you fail to give them any thought; but the good of the past is always there, ready to give you a continuing blessing, when you take time to remember.

All good relationships carry so many rich treasures with them that we can find much more to appreciate than we realize. So, although we may have difficult times of adjustment, we can always enrich our consciousness by giving thanks for the good we have shared, the happiness that no one can ever take away. Nothing is lost in Spirit.

A very difficult time in many lives is the experience of divorce. There may be a great sense of loss, a feeling of failure, and perhaps a sense of guilt and recrimination. Even *the years which the swarming locust has eaten* can be restored with a new and happier life than ever, when we are willing to receive our good. We can only do this by concentrating on the present moment, building for the future, and releasing the past. The most devastating experience in a person's life can produce its particular blessing, but only when the person stops thinking loss and starts thinking opportunity and growth. It is another of those overcomings that takes place deep inside the individual and produces fruit on every level.

This idea of getting rid of the thought of loss is based on one of the essential laws of mind: One thought must be dissolved before another can take its place.

Certainly the best way to overcome loss is to replace it with some good. We can do this only when we are willing to accomplish it first in our thoughts. Letting go of the memory of a deprivation is a small price to pay for all the abundance that awaits you as a child of God!

Don't believe that anyone or anything can keep your good from you.

Many times we feel a sense of loss because it seems that someone or a certain situation has the power to deprive us of the good we seek. It may be money. It may be love. Or it may be opportunity. But no person and no condition can withhold from us that which is our due when we stop looking to the outer appearances and start concentrating on the inner causes. That which is ours in Spirit is eternally ours and can never be taken away.

We are the ones who give to others and to situations the power to hold us back. If we believe it, it is so! At least it becomes so for us so long as we hold on to the mistaken impression. So long as we believe that certain people are standing in our way, we will fail to see the many other paths to our goal. We will allow ourselves to be held back by our own sense of loss and deprivation.

But when we decide to break out of the thought that anyone or anything can keep our good from us, we also break out of the conditions that seemed to hold us back.

Usually the thought of loss, based on the ability of seemingly very real conditions to withhold our good, is sustained by a feeling of fear—fear of breaking loose, fear of what another person will do or say, or even fear of being on our own or entering into an unknown area. So many thoughts can hold us back, and none of them belongs to us as children of God! When we are in tune with God and following His guidance in all things, we may be sure that even the impossible becomes possible, because there is no impossibility in Spirit.

On occasion, people feel that in some way they will always hold themselves back from some opportunity or some greater good. Their sense of loss is the result of feeling that they are, as they will tell you, their "own worst enemy."

If this ever happens to you, remind yourself that you have just begun to know your possibilities and potentialities. You are wonderful! You are a child of God. Only in your mind, in your failure to appreciate and develop all that you are in Spirit—only there can you hold yourself back from the richer, fuller life God has for you. Let go of the lost self-esteem and start building the new image of yourself as God's expression—courageous, free, and fulfilled. You have all you can ever need of courage and ability right within you now.

Do forgive yourself and others.

Many times the thought of loss and the resulting experience of seeming deprivation are rooted in unforgiveness or resentment. We cannot reap our greater good until we have cleansed these deep-rooted feelings.

Remembering that no one and no thing have the power to withhold our good, we can go forward immediately in wonderful ways, once we have freed ourselves from the thoughts that continue to hold us in the limitations of the past. One of the strongest error emotions is the feeling of resentment and anger. It may be perpetuated for years, continuing to rob those involved of rich blessings and opportunities. We can't afford unforgiveness—of ourselves or of others.

Frequently the cause of a sense of loss and limitation is a person's feeling that he or she has failed in the past and consequently cannot succeed in the present. This thought is a perpetuation of a mistake that can keep those swarming locusts in mind constantly, destroying the present crops that could produce an abundant harvest of good if we were simply willing to let them grow. We must forgive ourselves, as well as others.

Forgiveness is a form of releasing that frees us to lay hold of the greater good that awaits. Always there are opportunities, no matter how many chances have seemingly been lost. Every day brings its own open doorways; and whenever we decide to release the wrongs of the past, whether we are blaming ourselves or others, we will be ready to lay hold of the good that the present moment brings. And what a wonderful opportunity that becomes! It is up to us, however, to choose whether we will continue to let those locusts gnaw away while we feel sorry for ourselves, or whether we will walk through the doorway of Truth into the new life God has for us—right now, here, today.

Of course, one part of forgiveness is forgetting. So we must also erase even the memory of the wrong. Then we will have plenty of room to expand the good ideas and unlimited blessings of the present moment, and all those moments to come.

Do fill your mind with thoughts of God's abundance.

Filling our minds with the realization of God's bounty will not only restore the outer blessings, with increase, but will also build a consciousness in us that will produce bountifully both the blessings of inner light and growth and the outer manifestations of abundant substance.

When Joel was talking to the Hebrews, he didn't promise them just a little. He drew word pictures to enable them to see with their inner vision a great abundance of good, a bountiful harvest. He made his promises specific and colorful. He spoke of rain in abundance (a necessity for good crops in a dry land). Then he said: *"The threshing floors shall be full of grain, the vats shall overflow with wine and oil."* (Joel 2:24) In other words, he was inviting the people to join him in imaging the rich harvest they wanted and needed. They were to forget the locusts and the trials of the past and concentrate on the bountiful crop they wanted to produce in the present. It was a lesson in positive thinking applied to the everyday life of the people.

Joel invited them to experience in advance (within their thinking-feeling nature) how it would feel to *"eat in plenty and be satisfied."* (Joel 2:26)

To prepare to receive the even greater good, once we have freed ourselves from all thought of loss, we too can use the power of our imagination. We should continually picture abundance.

When we open our purses, we can bless the money that is there and picture the pocketbook filled to overflowing. When we look around at nature, we can try to count the leaves on the trees, or the snowflakes, depending on the climate and the time of the year. We can look out at the heavens and contemplate the many worlds beyond our own, planets and suns much larger than ours.

While we fill our imaginations with pictures of abundance, we can affirm: *God is abundance,* or, *God is prosperity, and I am prosperity.*

As we become busy and interested, expanding our vision into infinity, we may notice, almost incidentally, that somehow we are attracting greater abundance in our material lives, enough and to spare, replacing and even surpassing that which we had before. Even more important, the locusts no longer inhabit and monopolize our thinking. They are gone, and with them their devastating effects on our lives.

We can then go even further. Getting in tune with God and His abundance does much more than increase our material prosperity. It also establishes in us a new and greater awareness of God at work, and it produces spiritual growth and understanding.

Joel predicted this too when he said: *"And it shall come to pass afterward, that I will pour out my spirit on all flesh; your sons and your daughters shall prophesy, your old men shall dream dreams, and your young men shall see visions."* (Joel 2:28)

When we are completely open to God's bounty and free from all thoughts of lack, loss, and limitation, we too will "prophesy" our own rich experiences. Not only that, but our vision will go beyond that which we have consciously chosen. We will begin to glimpse greater and greater good, and we will let ourselves become channels to attract it and express it. We will be a blessing not only to ourselves, but to others as well. And we will praise God *"who has dealt wondrously"* with us.

And as we continue to utilize divine ideas

and spiritual insight, we will find that our material surroundings are filled with God's love and goodness. Truly, nothing is ever lost in Spirit. When we turn away from loss and give our loving attention back to God, we find that God has given us riches beyond measure—in mind and in manifestation. We are rich, right now!

How to Win Without Fighting

Fighting—mentally, physically, or through strategic maneuvering in a battle of wits—is the way of the world.

To many people, the practical approach to business involves tactics designed to get the best of competitors. While they may not actually indulge in fisticuffs, their strategy may be plotted specifically to undercut a competitor's price, discredit another company, or even, in some way, to steal the secrets of a more successful business.

In many areas today, individuals are "fighting for their rights," spending a great deal of time and money in attempts to wrest from others what they feel is their due. This may take the form of a battle for position, money, love, or simply respect.

More than one person, wise in the world's way, will say to another, "It's a jungle out there!" or "It's dog eat dog. You have to fight!"

But no one ever wins a fight. Even the one who is victor in a particular skirmish will at some time be challenged by another, stronger opponent. The person who chooses to fight his or her way through life will have to do just that, and sooner or later will lose. That is the way of resistance.

There is a better way. It is not only a more effective way of accomplishing good results; it is a method that is tried and true, having been proved time and again in Bible stories. It is possible to win without fighting. Not only that, but the results can be more wonderful than anything that could possibly have been attained through human methods alone.

Consider the story of Jehoshaphat, the king of Judah. His country was invaded by a coalition made up of the Ammonites, Moabites, and the inhabitants of Mount Seir. Militarily, the people of Judah were no match for the combined armies of these three neighboring tribes.

An advocate of military might and human rights could easily have advised them what to do. In spite of their obvious inadequacy from a material viewpoint, they might have been urged to frenzied preparation for a fight to the death, using whatever material means were available. Or they would have been called to strategy sessions to determine some way to take advantage of the weaknesses of the enemy.

This is, of course, the way many people today prepare to fight the battles of the marketplace or the courtroom.

Jehoshaphat, who was, on the whole, a good king, called the people together to seek a better way. They reacted as the Jewish people did over and over whenever they were faced by the problem of strong enemies approaching with armies. They came together to pray. From all over Judah, they converged on the temple in Jerusalem where Jehoshaphat led them in prayer.

Not only did he lead them in prayer, but Jehoshaphat, who in a human way was very much afraid of the vast multitude of the opposing army, called for a fast throughout the kingdom.

Jehoshaphat in his public prayer talked about the situation to God as he would to a friend. Then he closed by saying: *"For we are powerless against this great multitude that is coming against us. We do not know what to do, but our eyes are upon thee."* (II Chron. 20:12)

From a human viewpoint, it is natural to be afraid at times and to recognize that one is no match for certain persons or conditions on the worldly plane. But when we, like Jehoshaphat, even recognizing the "facts" of the case, are willing to look to God for our deliverance, we will find, as he did, that there are ways where, to our limited human sight, there appear to be none.

There was a silence after Jehoshaphat finished speaking, and then one of the people of Judah, a man named Jahaziel, began to prophesy, relaying the words of God that he was hearing. His first words, as from the Lord, were an admonition not to be afraid because of the great multitudes. He even told where to find the opposing armies. Jahaziel added: " 'You will not need to fight in this battle; take your position, stand still, and see the victory of the Lord on your behalf, O Judah and Jerusalem.' Fear not, and be not dismayed; tomorrow go out against them, and the Lord will be with you." (II Chron. 20:17)

Note that Jahaziel did not recommend either of the alternatives to fighting that many people would choose. He didn't suggest running away from the danger, and he didn't recommend surrender to the enemy. He did advocate taking a stand with God, which might seem impractical from a human viewpoint, but which, in this case, turned out to be the most practical approach to the problem.

114

Jehoshaphat had the reassurance he needed and the instruction as well. So early the next morning, he led his people out into the wilderness of Tekoa. He spoke strong words of encouragement, and he appointed singers to precede the people, praising God and giving thanks for His love, which would deliver them.

As the group advanced, those who had been allied against Judah began to fight each other for no apparent reason. By the time the people of Judah reached the *watchtower of the wilderness,* (II Chron. 20:24) the opposing armies had annihilated each other, and all that was left for them to do was to collect the spoils of war. They didn't have to fight at all, and they returned to Jerusalem, still giving thanks to God.

Many times the Israelites were delivered from powerful enemies — not by fighting, but by trusting in God to lead them in the right way and to do for them whatever they were unable to do for themselves. Always there was some responsibility the children of Israel had to assume, something that they had to do to bring about the right result. But once they did their part, God did the rest.

It was not their place to tell God how to solve their problems. Instead, they prayed first; and when they received the guidance as to what they were to do, they followed it, trusting

God to bring about the right result. And He did, sometimes in ways that seemed to be totally impractical, or even supernatural. Who would have thought that three powerful armies, banded together to conquer another country, would start fighting among themselves and annihilate each other? Many times God's ways involve answers that we could never discover in our human searching.

Frequently too we find that those worldly powers and competitive people we fear have within themselves the seeds of their own destruction.

The Moabites, Ammonites, and inhabitants of Mount Seir stand for human attitudes that may be powerful when allowed to take command, but which can annihilate themselves when we are willing to turn to God and withdraw from them all the power of our thoughts and feelings.

Both the Ammonites and the Moabites were the descendants of Lot, Abraham's selfish and willful nephew, and his daughters. Metaphysically, the Ammonites stand for: *Popular opinion; also the wild, uncultivated states of consciousness that thoughts of sensuality, sin, and ignorance have formed in the outer world.* You cannot be "one of the crowd" and accept the dictates of popular worldly practices without giving power to the Ammonites.

The Moabites have some good in them, as they represent our thoughts; but they involve too much emphasis on the body and the *external conditions of life.*

The people of Mount Seir relate to the *physical or sense consciousness in man.*

Understanding this symbology, we can see why in our spiritual ongoing we cannot allow these invaders to conquer our thoughts and feelings. We do not win over them by fighting, because it is always difficult to rout out insidious demands of the body and threatening attitudes of public opinion. The only way we can cope with them is by looking to a higher power, by looking to God for deliverance and following the guidance He gives. We can win without fighting! These false concepts can be all around us, but they won't hurt us when we are keeping our thoughts firmly on God and good.

Here are some "dos" and "don'ts" for winning the battles of everyday life without fighting.

Don't be afraid.

We, with Jehoshaphat, must recognize that fear is an emotion we simply cannot afford. We must know too that we can overcome it. We do not have to live with fear; and we won't when we learn to work with the one Power that is greater than public opinion, greater than threatening circumstances, and greater even than the conflict that sometimes goes on inside us.

When Jehoshaphat first heard of the approaching armies and was afraid, he *proclaimed a fast throughout all Judah.* (II Chron. 20:3) So we, when we first are confronted with a situation that causes us to become fearful and anxious, must learn to fast from thoughts of the threat or danger and turn to the One who can provide the answer. We never solve our problems by looking at all the dangers in the world or even by consulting all our friends to find out what we should do. (We may find that we have as many alternatives as we have friends to tell us about them.)

There is only One who knows the answer that is right for us. There is only One who can show us the better way. And that is the Spirit of God within us. But how can we hear Him if our inner world is filled with fear and hate, frustration and anger? We cannot listen to God's voice if we are busily demanding that He do our will in handling the situation.

We need to fast from fear in order to listen and obey. We need to turn away from the situation, no matter how great the threat it seems to carry. We must turn within. There is no other way to find the right and perfect answer.

A good thought to take with us into the within of ourselves is: . . . *he who is in you is greater than he who is in the world,* (I John 4:4) the reassuring words of John. We can make them even more personal by facing down any fear with the affirmation: *Greater is He who is within me than he who is in the world.*

When Jehoshaphat turned to God in prayer, one of the first things he was told was: " 'Fear not, and be not dismayed at this great multitude.' " (II Chron. 20:15) Clearly and continually the Bible reveals to us that we, as children of God with instant access to His help, are not to be afraid.

Remember that you choose the situations that will have power in your life when you choose your thoughts and feelings about them. Learn to turn off the fear. Learn to fast from feeling afraid, and you will take command over your life.

Don't fight mentally, physically, or spiritually.

Nonresistance is one of the most powerful weapons we have, but it is too rarely used. Many who would spurn actual physical conflict or questionable competitive business practices still feel that it is natural to resist mentally, to fight each battle in thoughts and words and

119

complaints. (Even complaining about a situation gets in the way of making contact with God in order to receive guidance as to the right way to handle it.)

If we are wasting ourselves in mental sparring with an imaginary foe, we have no might to cope with the conditions of our lives. We must reserve our strength for higher purposes if we are to be triumphant, regardless of what comes to us to be handled. We cannot afford mental resistance!

The gunfighters of the Old West are a prime example of the futility of physical resistance. The greater the reputation a fighter had, the more he had to defend himself against all challengers, until one day someone else became the new champion. Physical resistance may be the way of the world, and it may work on a short-range basis, but in the long run it wages a losing fight.

There is a difference between taking a stand, as the people of Judah did, and fighting a battle. Nonresistance doesn't imply that we are to do nothing. It means, rather, that we are to direct our energies to the positive results we want to achieve.

If you have been accustomed to fighting, standing up for your rights, and generally adopting a belligerent attitude, you may find that this new method requires a complete program of mind retraining. It is easy to be carried away by the old customary reaction. So you must start to watch your thoughts and your feelings carefully, reprogramming yourself to stop and think before you ruffle your feathers and brace for a confrontation.

Even those mental habits of automatically taking offense at another's words or actions must be changed. Jealousy, criticism, and affront so cloud your mind that you cannot see clearly to find the right solution to any problem or situation.

And if you feel that you "can't help" losing your temper or fighting back, remember Jehoshaphat. He didn't become upset and rant and rave about the enemies. He didn't try to hide from the opposing armies. Neither did he rush about trying to stir up resistance against the invaders. Instead, he marshalled all his forces for prayer. And so can we.

Do look to God first.

Jehoshaphat not only took time out to pray himself, but he called all his people together to join him in looking to God first. When many leaders would have been busy checking on arms and trappings of war, he was spending time, effort, and energy seeking God's guidance and direction. Regardless of appearances,

121

he sought God first.

He had the human feelings many would have under those circumstances when he declared in his prayer: *"We do not know what to do, but our eyes are upon thee."* (II Chron. 20:12) Then he waited until God's answer came.

Many people rush into prayer to tell God about their problems, then run back out into the world without ever hearing what the Lord might have to say to them. But Jehoshaphat waited, and he was rewarded by instruction as to what he should do to handle the crisis.

God will do as much for us, regardless of the situation that confronts us. When we look to Him, He will provide the answer we seek. He can't do it when we are rushing around in a frenzy trying to cope with a lot of things—not because He doesn't have the answer at that time, but because we can't hear it. We have to pay attention if we want to receive God's direction. We must look to Him first. Then it is up to us to follow through on His guidance.

Do "'... take your position, stand still, and see the victory of the Lord...'" (II Chron. 20:17)

First we pray. Then we follow through on our prayer. As James said: *So faith by itself, if it has no works, is dead.* (James 2:17) Whatever God instructs us to do we must do.

Many times we may be unable to see what good results can be accomplished by following through on the guidance we receive. At such times we can remember Jehoshaphat. Would any "practical" person expect to vanquish three armies by going out to meet them with singing? To all human reasoning, our instructions may seem ridiculous. But God's ways are above the ways of the human, and, when we learn to trust Him and to do it anyway, we will see that it works — in expected or unexpected ways.

And what is the "position" we must take? It is the position of believing so completely in God that we are willing to do whatever He tells us to do. Not only that, but we do it willingly, freely, and with thanksgiving.

Although Jehoshaphat had been told that his people would not have to fight, he was instructed to lead them out against the enemy anyway. That took faith — to believe so completely in God's promise that they went willingly and freely toward the danger, trusting in God's deliverance.

As the Jewish people did many times in emergencies, they went forth singing and praising God. And it was after they had begun to sing and praise that the other tribes began to fight each other.

Sometimes we have to see God's guidance all the way through before we begin to get recognizable results. We may have to prove our faith utterly as we take the position that has been assigned to us and stand firm on the Truth that we know as we await results. But we can win without fighting. We can, when we are willing to trust God all the way.

A particularly important part of the action of the people of Judah in this story was their willingness to give thanks in advance, before they had seen any outer results. Instead of waiting for God to deliver their enemies into their hands, they took the Lord at His word and went forward in perfect confidence, knowing that, in the right way at the right time, whatever was necessary would be done. It might have been that they would have to do something more, but if so, they would have been ready and would have followed through on the next step. This too is part of the process of winning— God's way.

It was when Jehoshaphat and the people reached *the watchtower of the wilderness* that they first saw the results of their prayer activity. Their prayer for deliverance had been answered; and not only that, but they reaped rich spoils as well.

Many of us go through wilderness experiences, times when we feel that our lives are barren and meaningless, but if we persist in following God's guidance all the way to the watchtower—the high spiritual awareness in which we are acting confidently—expecting right results, we will find our answer.

How can we take the position God has for us at this time? How can we see God's victory in our lives? After looking to Spirit first, we can follow whatever guidance we receive. It may mean making a telephone call. It may mean turning down a certain street, or contacting a particular person. It may simply mean resting and trusting quietly in God. Whatever God tells us to do, let us do it with thanksgiving, praising Him and knowing that all things are working out for good.

When we do, we will find that truly it is possible to win without fighting. We may even discover that all the challenges we faced eliminated each other when we stopped looking at them and giving them the power of our faith.

How to Get Rid of Excess Weight

Many people today go through life carrying heavy burdens that they feel are necessary to life as they know it.

Others allow themselves to be slaves to more than enough money and possessions. Still others experience the heaviness of being overweight in mind and body but feel powerless to do anything about it.

There are also those who go through life burdened by thoughts of guilt and anger, feelings of deprivation and pain.

It is not necessary to carry excess weight of mind, body, or possessions through life. When we learn to adjust our life experiences to the pattern given by Jesus Christ, we will find that divine adjustment also takes place in our minds, bodies, and affairs.

Even in the mental area, there are certain methods we can use to make our bodies slim and beautiful, our minds and emotions peaceful and happy, and our affairs a reflection of the divine order that is making its home within us. We can get rid of excess weight!

The Bible teaching on this subject is clear, and there are many applications we can make of the basic principles taught.

The rich young man who approached Jesus on one occasion is a good example. Like many people today, he thought he wanted to learn the Master's way, but when it came right down to it, he discovered that he was too attached to the material side of living. He wasn't willing to give up any part of his comfortable life in order to grow and develop in a spiritual way, not even to follow the Man whom he admired so much.

If we want to become slim in body, free in mind, and unencumbered in our daily living, we must be willing to make a commitment that goes beyond the wish of the man who approached Jesus.

This well-dressed gentleman ran up to Jesus and knelt before Him to ask: "... *Good Teacher, what must I do to inherit eternal life?*" (Mark 10:17)

The Master spoke of the Ten Commandments given by Moses, and the young man, apparently well-read and of high position, quickly replied: "... *Teacher, all these I have observed from my youth.*" (Mark 10:20) He had been brought up in the Jewish faith where strict observance of these universal laws was emphasized as a part of religious training.

Jesus, with His usual insight into character, knew exactly where the young man's problem lay; and it is interesting to note that the Scripture says that, while perceiving the man's weakness, Jesus still *loved him.*

The Master said: "... *You lack one thing; go, sell what you have, and give to the poor, and you will have treasure in heaven; and come, follow me.*" (Mark 10:21) He hadn't told Matthew, the wealthy tax collector, to sell all he had; but perhaps He didn't have to. He hadn't told the hardy fishermen to get rid of their boats and their nets. But on this occasion He did point out that, if he would inherit the kingdom, the rich young man would have to give up his material wealth, which was very important to him.

Perhaps this man couldn't imagine life without the comforts and extravagances to which he was accustomed. Apparently he was expecting some quick and easy route to eternal life, maybe even something he could purchase with his money. But if so, he was certainly disappointed. Crestfallen, he walked away, as the

Bible story says, *for he had great possessions.* (Mark 10:22) Did he really have great possessions, or could it be that he was possessed by the money and things he thought he owned?

At any rate, Jesus took advantage of the incident to teach a lesson to the disciples. He pointed out: *"How hard it will be for those who have riches to enter the kingdom of God!"* (Mark 10:23) This comment surprised the disciples, who were accustomed to seeing the Master equally at home with the wealthy and learned men and with the penniless lepers. So Jesus went on to explain: *". . . Children, how hard it is to enter the kingdom of God! It is easier for a camel to go through the eye of a needle than for a rich man to enter the kingdom of God."* (Mark 10:24, 25)

The disciples felt that this constituted a condemnation of all who had material wealth, and they asked who could be saved. Jesus replied: *". . . With men it is impossible, but not with God; for all things are possible with God."* (Mark 10:27)

If we take these words of Jesus at their face value, we might find some justification for the contention that the Bible condemns money and riches and suggests poverty as the spiritual way. But this is not true.

Perhaps the key to the situation was that the

rich young man had more trust in his great wealth than in God's ability to provide for his needs. How, then, could he expect to enter the realm of divine ideas within him to which trust in God is the key?

The example of the camel and the needle's eye is a little more difficult to explain. It is hard to imagine anyone attempting to force a hump-backed camel through the eye of a needle, no matter how large the needle. Some authorities feel that this was simply Jesus' way of injecting a little humor into the teaching, with one of those colorful Eastern expressions that would bring a smile to the faces of the listeners.

One translator (George Lamsa), going back to the Aramaic word, changes "camel" to cable or rope and explains that a very small rope could be passed through a very large needle.

Another theory tells of a small postern gate beside the large city gate in Jerusalem called the "Needle's Eye." A loaded camel could go through the gate, but only on its knees, according to this theory. This, too, presents a ludicrous picture.

But let us consider the idea that the camel could go through the gate (if, in fact, there was such a gate), provided the load was removed. Perhaps this is the answer.

It is not possible for us to enter the kingdom

of God, the Christ consciousness, while loaded down with thoughts of our possessions or anything else of the material realm only. It is necessary for us to let go of the weights and burdens of material thinking and material living in order to enter that inner awareness that identifies completely with our spiritual nature.

Unity cofounder Charles Fillmore explains it this way:

Let us do away with the erroneous idea that men must be poor to be righteous. Money is man's instrument, not his master. Money was made for man, not man for money. Only those who put money above man and give it power in their minds by worshiping it are the "rich" men to whom Jesus referred in His story about the camel and the needle's eye. It is not money that controls men, but the ideas they have about money. Ideas of poverty are just as powerful to enslave men as are ideas of wealth.

We must learn to trust—not in the things we possess, but in the intangible reality of God and His goodness. Jesus was not condemning wealth as such, but the idea of being possessed by it—the consciousness that looks to the material world first and to God last. When we look first to God, all things will be put in their proper perspective; and we will have the necessary things, as Jesus said, as a result of seeking first the kingdom of God ideas.

Even in talking about the rich man entering the kingdom of God, Jesus pointed to the way of grace by his closing words: " . . . *all things are possible with God."* (Mark 10:27)

But what does all this have to do with being burdened or overweight or unhappy? A study of Jesus' teachings gives us some "dos" and "don'ts" to apply in getting rid of excess weight, whether it is in the form of extra padding on the body, burdensome thoughts and feelings, or frustrations with material possessions.

Don't hoard things or thoughts.

The whole idea of hoarding is wrapped up with thoughts of future lack and limitation. One who hoards money accumulates and stores away his cash in the expectation that someday he will need it. In many cases, he is mentally projecting a future emergency for which the money is required. Or he may simply fear the loss of it, in which case he will surely attract loss into his life. Many times that which is hoarded is hidden, which indicates a certain furtiveness along with the fear and anxiety.

As far as material wealth is concerned, the possession of money and houses and lands may or may not limit spiritual growth. It may or may not prove to be a burden. It may or may not be

133

the "excess weight" that must be eliminated from the productive life. It all depends on the owner's attitude toward it. Even those who have little may be burdened with thoughts of money, selfishness with what they have, and envy of people who have more. These mental encumbrances may be even more costly than the rich man's preoccupation with his wealth. Certainly neither situation is healthy nor productive.

As Charles Fillmore pointed out: *It is not a crime to be rich nor a virtue to be poor* . . . . The "crime," if there is one, lies in the thoughts and feelings that are related to the possessions or lack of them.

Frequently those who are overweight in body are people who hoard things. I have known people who kept complete wardrobes in several sizes. When they gained weight, they moved up through the various sizes. Then, as they dieted, they went the other way, working their way down to smaller clothes. But they always kept the larger ones, because they were sure it wouldn't last—they couldn't remain slim. And pretty soon they were wearing those carefully hoarded large sizes again.

If you have had a problem with being overweight, perhaps it would be well for you to check the attic and the closets. Is there something there you should release? There is nothing like a good housecleaning (including closets, attic, basement, and garage, all of those catch-alls) to give you a feeling of lightness. And when you feel light in mind and body, pretty soon your body will express it.

Overweight people also may have a tendency to hold on to thoughts and feelings that should be released. There may be old resentments and a tendency to blame others for troubles.

Many times individuals overeat in an attempt to satisfy a feeling of frustration. But they only succeed in becoming more frustrated and unhappy with themselves. There are other, better ways to get rid of frustrations.

Sometimes people eat too much because they are bored. Not being actively interested in anything, they pass the time by eating—and add excessive burdens they can ill afford.

Even those weight problems that are caused by gland imbalance can be cured by thoughts of release, freedom, and interest in life.

There is no place for hoarding in the life of one who would get rid of excess weight, whether it is the hoarding of material things or of old, outworn thoughts and feelings.

We are all supposed to live richly. We are designed to enjoy the material things that will contribute to our lives and growth. There is nothing wrong with savings accounts, if they are established for good purposes with the right thoughts in mind. But none of us can afford to hoard—things or thoughts.

Remember, you will be weighted down by anything that inhibits your progress—morally, mentally, physically, or spiritually.

Do decide to take control of your life.

When the rich young man turned down the opportunity to get rid of his wealth and accompany Jesus, studying with the Master, he was saying, in effect, "I can't help it. In many ways I would like to, but I just can't give up the way I've been living."

Today many people are also saying, as an excuse for everything from worrying about money to continual overeating, "I can't help it!"

But we can help it! We can overcome any bad habit, whether it is physical or mental, when we decide to take control over our thoughts, feelings, bodies, and affairs. We are not the victims of circumstances or appetites. We are not supposed to bow down to obsessions of the mind or cravings of the body. We are spiritual beings, and we are designed to live joyously and freely.

Never say you "can't help" remembering past injustices. You can forgive if you want to be freed from the burden of unforgiveness. And you will, when you are willing to take the necessary control.

Never say you can't help worrying or you can't help being depressed or anxious or fearful. You can—when you are willing to start acting like the child of God you are created to be.

As for eating those extra sweets and starches that put the excess pounds on your body—that too can be overcome when you decide to take control.

One time I was counseling with a very large woman who had decided she wanted to lose weight. I suggested that she try "treasure-mapping"—cutting out pictures of people with the type of figure she wanted to have and pasting them on a colored cardboard, which she kept handy in the kitchen near the refrigerator. She was to paste a snapshot of her head on the body and to look at the picture, visualize herself slim, and give thanks to God for the realization of her dreams.

It was working! She found that actually she was losing her desire for rich foods and beginning to take off weight. Then one day she went out to lunch. Out of habit, she ordered a rich dessert. When it came, she was surprised to realize that she simply didn't want it. But she made herself eat it anyway! And pretty soon she was back where she had started. As long as she took control of her thinking through prayer, even the pictured prayer of the treasure map, she was getting rid of that excess weight; but when she let the old habits take over and control her, she lost the battle. It was her choice. And our lives are always our choice. We can be victims of habits, moods, material things, and the lures of food, tobacco, or alcohol, or we can decide to express the dominion God gave us in the beginning.

It's not enough to wish to be slim or to think it would be nice to get rid of old worries and other burdensome thoughts and feelings. We must continually choose what we really want and want it enough to work for it. There is no other way!

Do you want the pleasure of a shapely, healthy body, or the temporary indulgence of appetite? Do you prefer the misery of holding on to old resentment and anger, or would you like to be happily living in the present, active and productive? The choice is yours—not a choice you make once and forget, but a continuing choice that is the basis of day to day living.

Do establish new and productive habits.

Nature abhors a vacuum, so we must replace the old, destructive habits with new, productive ones. Otherwise, the old burdens will be back in charge before we realize what is happening.

Had the woman who wanted to be slim followed through by consciously choosing less fattening foods and developing a taste for them, she could have continued her progress until she matched the picture on her treasure map.

An occasional diet won't do it, whether you would like to get rid of excess pounds on the body or heavy, burdensome thoughts and feelings. It requires constant vigilance and a whole new way of thinking. Other measures alone will never be successful.

Many people go through life as though they were riding a ferris wheel, with ups and downs over which they seem to have no control. This is the result of letting themselves be controlled by people, things, and circumstances instead of consciously establishing the habits of thinking, speaking, and acting that will lead to the type of results they really want in their lives.

We can be happy, well, and healthy. We can be free and fulfilled. We can be whatever size we want to be. But first, we must see ourselves that way. As we establish new habits of thinking and feeling, expressing those ideas we most want to express, we will find that the old burdens and even the excess pounds just melt away.

We can take a lesson from the rich young man. He wasn't willing to change in order to follow Jesus Christ. But we will find that the rewards of following our own inner Christ—God's Spirit in us—are far greater than anything we give up when we release whatever excess weight we may have been carrying through life. And the new habits we establish in thought and feeling will lead us into rich and successful living, without burdens of mind, body, or possessions.

How to Remove Obstacles

Jesus' promise that mountains could be moved by even a small amount of faith has brought much comment and conjecture over the years.

Many people have applied the teaching literally to the moving of mountains made of earth and stone. And we find that such mountains can be moved by a certain amount of faith, backed up by manpower and ideas.

Even in ancient times it was possible to move mountains—or to make a mountain—if the desire was there. My husband and I once visited ancient Indian mounds near St. Louis. After making the long and strenuous climb to the top of one mound, we visited an information center, where we were told that these hills had been made by Indians carrying baskets of earth on their heads.

Thinking of the knoll we had just climbed,

we tried to imagine these early people going through that climb over and over, each time carrying a basket of dirt. Even harder to imagine were the patience, the dedication, the faith, and the perseverance of the many people who must have been involved. How many years it must have taken, with such difficult labor, to form the mountain of earth! And, of course, if mountains can be made by transporting small amounts of dirt at a time, then certainly they can be moved in the same way. It would take considerable manpower and time, but it could be done.

In more recent times, faith and large earth-moving equipment have literally transformed mountains into any shape desired. Some have been removed. Others have been bored for tunnels or mines. So, from a physical viewpoint, we can see that it is by no means impossible to move a substantial, physical mountain.

But there are other mountains that must be moved if we are going to live happy and productive lives. And these are the monstrous piles of rubbish and dirt that we may have allowed to accumulate in our thinking-feeling nature. These mountains serve as obstacles to the attaining of our hearts' desires, and in many cases they become seemingly immovable objects in our paths toward greater good.

Whenever we see some obstruction in our way, some hindrance that seems to be keeping us from the good we seek, then it is time to stop and take stock of our own thinking and also to learn a lesson from the teachings of Jesus.

The obstruction may involve the attitude of another person which seems to give that person the power to withhold our good or to keep us from doing something we feel is right.

It may be in the form of an illness, an accident, or some other difficulty that apparently leaves us incapacitated in a physical way, at an impasse in our lives.

Or, it may be in the form of our own thoughts about a certain situation. If we feel that we are going to be held back in some way, for instance, we may be confronting our own feelings of inadequacy or inferiority, throwing our own mental impediments in our path.

It doesn't really matter what the mountain situation may be or what the obstacle is. The principle taught by Jesus will enable us to displace the wrong thoughts and feelings that may be supporting the limitation; and when the support is gone, the impediment will remove itself from our lives.

Let us look at the occasion when Jesus gave the disciples the example of a small amount of faith in moving mountains.

The Master had climbed to a high place accompanied by three disciples, Peter, James, and John, for this mountaintop experience.

There Jesus . . . *was transfigured before them, and his face shone like the sun, and his garments became white as light.* (Matt. 17:2) Jesus was in a very high spiritual awareness, and the three who were praying with Him were able to see beyond their normal vision to the spiritual reality. This time they were *heavy with sleep,* but when they awoke, they beheld Jesus in His radiant body and also envisioned Moses and Elijah talking with Him. It was a glorious experience for them, and they would have liked to have stayed on the mountain and built three temples there. But they had to return to the world of everyday activity, taking with them the memory of the spiritual experience.

When they reached the foot of the mountain, where the rest of the disciples and a crowd awaited them, they were quickly reminded of mundane matters.

A man whose son was an epileptic came to Jesus and asked Him to heal the boy. He pointed out: *"I brought him to your disciples, and they could not heal him."* (Matt. 17:16)

As the child was being brought to Jesus, he had an attack of epilepsy, but even this did not affect Jesus, who . . . *rebuked the unclean spirit, and healed the boy, and gave him back to his father.* (Luke 9:42)

When they had a chance to talk to Him privately, the disciples asked Jesus why they had not been able to cure the boy. Earlier in His ministry He had sent the twelve out in twos with the instruction: *"Heal the sick, raise the dead, cleanse lepers, cast out demons."* (Matt. 10:8) And they had been able to accomplish great works in His name. So naturally they wondered what had gone wrong this time.

Jesus answered simply: *"Because of your little faith."* (Matt. 17:20) Then He went on with the great teaching: *"For truly, I say to you, if you have faith as a grain of mustard seed, you will say to this mountain, 'Move from here to there,' and it will move; and nothing will be impossible to you."* (Matt. 17:21) So far as we know, none of the disciples ever did try to move a mountain, but they had received one more lesson that would stand them in good stead when Jesus was no longer with them in the physical body.

Even a small amount of faith would enable them to be channels for mighty works. As they all knew, the mustard seed was very small, but it had within it the potential of a sizable tree. Even a little faith, tiny as a mustard seed, could become the force that would move any mountain from their lives.

Many times people feel that Jesus would not have understood the problems we face today, obstacles that might seem monstrous and impossible to move. But when we study the life of Jesus, we find that He had to cope with all sorts of difficulties, antagonistic people, and even physical threats. But, no matter what the obstacle, He was not only able to handle it but to come out triumphant in the end. And so can we.

Jesus, early in His ministry, faced the temptations of giving up His high ideals and aspirations in order to have power, fame, human acclaim, and physical satisfaction. And He satisfactorily removed these obstacles from His path to spiritual growth and realization.

Certainly it was not easy during His ministry to cope with the challenge of being highly acclaimed by large groups of people at one moment, and then accosted by others who were seeking to not only discredit His teaching, but even to take His life.

There were many obstacles. No matter what He did, He was likely to be criticized by those in authority. And it was not unusual for the multitude who followed Him in the good times to desert Him when things got tough. Even the disciples were not eager to be associated with

Him when He was arrested and taken before the Sanhedrin. Three times within a short period of time before dawn Peter, one of the three who were closest to Him, denied knowing Him.

So Jesus knew what it was to have challenges. He was well acquainted with obstacles set in His path. But, through it all, He sought inner guidance for correctly handling all situations, and He triumphed. If we will follow His way, we can remove any impediment from our paths.

His teachings can be applied to the moving of any mountain, whether it is a mental block that keeps you from your good or some person or situation in your path that presents a seemingly real and immovable obstacle.

Here are some "dos" and "don'ts" for moving the mountains that stand in your way.

Don't let the illusion fool you.

As we were traveling in the western part of the United States several years ago, we saw many signs pointing out the Lewis and Clark trail, the route followed by those two well-known adventurers and their party of exploration.

In Montana, as we were driving toward Glacier National Park, we came to a place where we first saw the Rocky Mountains, very much as the explorers may have first seen them. These enormous, craggy, grayish peaks stretched all the way across the horizon and, as we looked at them, there seemed to be no possible way through. Here was certainly an obstacle that seemed forbidding and immovable.

Very soon after we first saw the mountains of the Continental Divide, dominating the distant landscape, we came to another marker on the Lewis and Clark trail. It pointed to "Camp Disappointment." This was the place where the Lewis and Clark expedition camped; and those hardy leaders, looking at the seemingly impenetrable barrier of rocky peaks, decided to turn back. As we know now, there are passes, ways through the mountains, in that stretch of the Rockies that the explorers surveyed from a distance. But apparently they were appalled by the obstacle and completely deceived by the illusion that there was no way through.

This can happen to you too, if you look at problems stretched across your horizon and declare, "It's impossible. It can't be done!" But it can. All it takes is the understanding that problems themselves are illusions, just situations in which there appears to be an absence of God. But bring God into the situation, learn to listen to His guidance and follow His direction, and you will find the way through your mountains.

There is always a pass. There is always a way. Don't let yourself be stopped by the illusions of Camp Disappointment!

Perhaps the disciples were unable to heal the child because they were deceived by the appearance. Maybe their faith was not great enough to block out the mental picture of a seizure as they called forth the perfect idea within.

It is easy to be deceived by the illusions of everyday life. Disease may appear very real. Lack may seem to dominate the landscape. Other people may appear to be very powerful in our lives.

But we must learn to declare to ourselves: *There is a way. With God there is always a way.* When we concentrate on finding the way, instead of being dominated by the illusion, we have made the first step toward removing any obstacle.

Do withdraw and recoup spiritually.

In one version of the story of Jesus, the disciples, and the epileptic child, we are told that Jesus, when asked why the disciples couldn't perform the healing, replied: *"This kind cannot be driven out by anything but prayer and fasting."* (Mark 9:29 A.V.)

Faith is built through prayer and denial, and sometimes the only way to resolve a particular

149

situation is to withdraw from outer activity and pray it all the way through. Fasting, of course, means withdrawing all power from negative thoughts and feelings, getting away from anything that might cut us off from our good in mind.

Prayer, by the same token, means filling our minds and hearts with positive, spiritual, uplifting ideas. Certainly we are better able to remove mountains when we are free from limiting thoughts and feelings and filled with joyous inspiration.

A friend of mine recently had the opportunity to confront and remove an obstacle from her life, and she used this principle.

She was teaching in a high school where violence had been rampant. There had been so much trouble that not only had security guards been hired, but city policemen were also stationed there.

In many ways she welcomed the teaching opportunities at the school because she felt that the students were very much in need of motivation and encouragement.

One day, when she corrected one of the teenage students, the girl became violently angry and started cursing her and acting in such a threatening manner that the teacher felt she must call in the assistant principal. Before it was over, one of the city policemen had to take the student home.

This was on Friday, and a short time later the teacher heard from the girl's mother. She was extremely angry and told my teacher friend that she was going to get a gun and shoot her. Within a short while she had spread the word that on Monday she would wait for the teacher in the parking lot and shoot her when she got out of her car. In most places this might have been considered an idle threat, but not in this school and this neighborhood.

The teacher, already upset by the incident with the student, was really unnerved by the mother's belligerence. But she decided she would have to work with the spiritual principles she knew. She had been beholding the Christ in the students and seeking to encourage them to do some goal-striving. Now she needed to do some intensive prayer work on herself, and also work on the girl and her mother. All weekend, whenever she thought of them, she denied the evidence of anger and mental disorder. She visualized God at work and saw both mother and daughter receptive to the activity of the Christ.

Monday and Tuesday passed without further incident, and she continued to give thanks to God. Wednesday morning the student returned to class and walked up to the teacher to apologize to her. And then, hesitantly, she asked, "Will you teach me how to keep from losing my temper like that?" The last I heard, she was sincerely trying to learn.

Sometimes there is no other way. In order to overcome a particular situation, or even just our thoughts about it, we must withdraw to that place within ourselves where we can thoroughly cleanse and revitalize our thinking-feeling nature. Fasting from all thought of the problem and feasting on spiritual ideas is the only way. But it works and will continue to work. Obstacles can be removed through prayer and fasting—first from within us and then from our paths.

Sometimes all it takes to move a mountain is to move ourselves—in the right direction. As we traveled through Glacier National Park and approached the Canadian Rockies, we were captivated by Chief Mountain, standing by itself, dominating the landscape.

A few miles and turns later, my husband suddenly joked, "Look, Chief Mountain has moved over there." Of course it quickly came to me, "The mountain didn't move, we did."

And sometimes when we have moved ourselves in thought, we find that is all that is necessary to change the whole perspective of any situation, to put that obstacle, mental or material, right out of our picture.

Do speak the word.

Even idle words, spoken without much thought or feeling, have some effect in our lives. But those words that we back up with strong emotion are bound to express in outer ways. That is why we must always be careful about our words and about the reinforcement we give them from our emotional depths.

By the same token, the words that are most powerful and effective are those that are spoken in the conviction of God as the one Presence and one Power in the universe, the one Reality in our lives. When we have prepared ourselves through mental cleansing and positive prayer activity, we are ready to speak the words that will get results, the commands that will move all obstacles in the way of our good.

Jesus frequently employed the power of the word to heal or to transform conditions. When the epileptic child was convulsed, He *rebuked the unclean spirit.* (Mark 9:25) We don't know just what words He used, but it doesn't matter. He spoke with all the authority of spiritual at-one-ment, and something happened!

When He talked about moving mountains, He recommended speaking to the mountain, using the power of the word backed up by faith to get results, to accomplish the good.

We too can speak the word of faith to the obstacles in our lives—not in the sense of fighting them or resisting them, but rather with the decision to be rid of them, to dismiss them from our lives, taking the authority over ourselves and our world that God gave us in the beginning.

After we have withdrawn from the world and prepared ourselves by *prayer and fasting,* then we are ready to speak the word of power, to remove the obstacle, to call forth the good, to go forth into the unlimited realm of answers and abundance.

What words should we use? God will tell us when we ask, in the silence of our own being, in the stillness where we are establishing our faith and building our relationship with Spirit. And when we speak those words, even though our faith may seem inadequate at first, it will grow, and we will grow, until we see that what appeared to be a mountain in our path is nothing after all.

How to Clear Up Confusion

Confusion may appear to be the result of outer events, things that happen to us or around us. It may seem to result from the disorderly habits of others or from a variety of information compiled from the input of other people.

Actually, though, whether confusion expresses as our own inability to make a decision, based on conflicting information, or a disorderly jumble of things in the hall closet, confusion does not begin outside us. It begins within us—in our own thinking—in our own expression of mind as it relates to other minds, things, and conditions.

We may decry the disorderly habits of another person or blame all our troubles on a situation in which we find ourselves. But confusion is based in our own thoughts and feelings and comes about because of our reaction to what is going on. If we would clear up confusion in our lives, whether we are considering mental or physical results, we must go back to the causes in mind.

In many cases the state of confusion around us, including the disorderly persons with whom we come in contact, is the direct result of the thoughts we are holding in mind. A change in our thoughts can effect a change in our surroundings.

But a mental change alone is not enough. We may think and think, apply all methods of reason, and still not come up with right answers. As a matter of fact, we may produce even greater confusion. But we can use our thinking ability to take us all the way back to God, and it is there that we find the light of Truth, the illumination that will set us free from all confusion.

When we finally come to the place where we can let the radiance of Spirit shine in and through our thinking, we find that we have the ability to establish order, harmony, and right relationships in all that concerns us.

But how can we do this? Let us take a lesson from the story in Genesis of a place named confusion, the allegory of the Tower of Babel. The Hebrew word "Babel" means: . . . *confusion; chaos; vanity; nothingness.* This *story in which people, things, and happenings have other meanings* may have been written, as many Bible authorities believe, to show how languages originated. But it also holds other lessons for us today, as we study it for its spiritual import.

In their migration the descendants of Noah found a plain where they decided to settle down and build a city. They made bricks and erected buildings and a tower *with its top in the heavens.* (Gen. 11:4) Then, according to the storyteller, who exhibited the anthropomorphic concept of God so common in Old Testament times, the Lord came down to look over the city, decided to put an end to the people's attempt to build a tower into the heavens, and so . . . *confused the language of all the earth; and . . . scattered them abroad over the face of all the earth.* (Gen. 11:9)

There are several important points to consider in this story. First of all, there was a common purpose in this undertaking. We are told that *the whole earth had one language and few words.* (Gen. 11:1) This unity resulted in an interchange of information and formed the basis for a joint effort. Many things can be accomplished when people band together with a common interest and start great projects. There was only one trouble. The common language in this case was the language of materiality. The people were basing their lives on the world of bricks and mortar. They spoke the same language because they were all interested in food, clothing, buildings, and luxuries — the material things that they felt were the most important part of life.

They had such great confidence in their intellectual planning and their materialistic building blocks that they even thought they could reach God through material means. That is why they started the tower.

Truly, great things have been accomplished in a unity of purpose, when people banded together to produce material marvels. But what of the great cities and civilizations of the past? Where are they now? Even before they were finished, many times the most ambitious projects deteriorated as individuals became separated by selfish interests and concerns. Other Babels?

Many people still speak the language of materiality; and they share this tongue with their friends, who also think in terms of money, possessions, and position as the building blocks of life. Some progress can be made in material areas, but sooner or later there is disappointment for one who lives in the worldly side alone. Even the greatest monument to vanity must sooner or later crumble away.

And people still try to build their contact with God through material means only. They follow certain rituals or say certain prayers without really putting themselves into an attitude of worship.

They may even give material gifts to God or to God's work as a substitute for giving themselves. There is nothing wrong with giving the gift (it is, or should be, a symbol of our trust in God's bounty), but the offering is not a substitute for our own thoughtful attention and dedication.

Undoubtedly a great contributing factor in the downfall of the people in Babel was an over-inflated personal ego. As they talked about building their city and their tower, they said: "... *let us make a name for ourselves.*" (Gen. 11:4) It was their desire to make a personal monument, establishing a great reputation throughout the world. They were like the Pharisees of Jesus' time who wore large phylacteries (cases containing Scriptural writings) on their foreheads and arms, and prayed in public, so that people would know how spiritual they were. Jesus said of them: "*They have received their reward.*" (Matt. 6:5)

Something else happens when people begin to work together in a spirit of self-interest. What starts out as the interest of the group soon becomes the selfish interest of the individual. If the project will reflect glory upon the whole group, how much more it will glorify the leader! Pretty soon, one moves to take charge and, of course, somebody else also wants to head the project. One would like to do it one way; somebody else has a better idea. Pretty soon the materialistic understanding becomes a mass of conflicting ideas and aims. Each person speaks a different language — the language of his particular self-interest. And when they no longer speak the same language, the people cannot communicate, and eventually they have to abandon what they started jointly with such high hopes and dreams.

The thought: "... *let us make a name for ourselves,*" may have started out as the desire to build a monument, the concept of providing a tourist attraction that would benefit the whole city. But it could only end up in a different kind of aim as each person began to have his own dreams of personal grandeur and selfish goals.

As we think of the mistakes of the people who were attempting to build Babel, we can see why their plan was doomed to failure. It was not the Lord in the phase of our loving heavenly Father who separated them, but their own mistaken dependence on worldly, material means alone. It was the action of God, working as law, that separated them. When there were the wrong motive and the wrong base of action, there had to be confusion. Success was impossible. Universal law always works, and it couldn't be otherwise.

All things were being done in a materialistic way with selfish purposes. The project had to fail—not because God was jealous or angry or anything else that the human being might feel, but because the thoughts and feelings of the people acted as causes that produced results under the law.

We find that many things can be accomplished by working in a unity of purpose in the common language of materiality; but, as with the Tower of Babel, they don't last.

Some people, recognizing this, try to go a little further and work with mental laws to get certain results in their lives. Again, up to a point, they can make progress. Many things can be accomplished through the power of the mind, operated on strictly a mental level; but, so long as personal aims and goals are the end, there comes a time of reckoning with the law. It is only the undertakings established on Spirit that are true and lasting. It is in our spiritual growth that we make true progress and build the lasting truths and values into our experience. These are the treasures we take with us from lifetime to lifetime. These are the valuables that never deteriorate and never grow old.

But what of the story's meaning for us? How can we use its lesson to clear up any confusion in our lives? Here are some "don'ts."

Don't let yourself be caught up in the confusion of the multitude.

The multitudes have a way of getting together and speaking one language. In most cases it is the language of materiality, the tongue of things and people and places, related solely to the world of bricks and mortar.

One form of a multitude speaking one language is the mob, a group of people banded together with a common purpose, one that is aimed toward destruction. It is easy to be drawn into mob action when emotion runs high and the leaders prey on pet prejudices or feelings of injustice. The group may speak a common language that leads them into action they would not take under ordinary circumstances. But we don't have to let ourselves be drawn into a mob or any other negative multitude speaking a language of the material world.

Neither must we respond to another kind of a multitude that speaks with one tongue. These disturbed voices loudly proclaim the current concerns from the daily news—high prices, shortages, and so on. From every grocery store and service station they cry, "Get upset with me!" It's your choice. You can join them and build a monster of confusion in your thoughts. Or you can decide to do your own thinking and choose your own attitudes and make your own world from within, not without.

The pressures are great from these voices because there is a certain strength in numbers, and there may be a strong unity of drive to make others join the common cause—the cause of complaint and fear and doubt. Many people join this group without ever realizing that they have made a choice. The plea is urgent, and those things that affect the pocketbook and the world of luxuries and even necessities occupy an important place in the lives of most people today.

But being different is always a part of the price we pay for spiritual growth and unfoldment. And if we would clear our thinking of confusion and establish our lives on a spiritual foundation, we have to learn to choose our own base of action.

It would have been difficult to converse with the early inhabitants of Babel with a different, spiritual approach. It may be difficult to talk to others today. But at least we can, within ourselves, choose the language we will speak and refuse to be simply caught up in the hysteria of the multitude.

Don't waste yourself on inconsequential matters.

The word "confuse" means *to mix up; jumble together; put into disorder.* When we fill our minds with a quantity of inconsequential matters, we will find that our thoughts become so mixed up, so jumbled, that it is difficult to sort them out. We lose all perspective as we allow inconsequential things to fall over each other in our thinking. In the long run, these questions and wonderings are totally unimportant, but for the moment we may so fill our minds with them that there is no room for the orderly considerations that will establish harmony in our actions and our relationships with others.

"Why did that happen?" "What did he mean by that?" "Was there something wrong there?" "Why don't things go the way I want them to?" "What's wrong with her?" "What's wrong with me?"

Around and around the queries go, and when it's all over, there are no answers—just a muddle of false information that causes confused conditions in our lives. We cannot argue out every small thought that comes and still expect to have orderly thinking and orderly conditions in our affairs. It just doesn't work that way.

The people of Babel must have been much concerned with small matters, inconsequential concerns of bricks and mortar. Unless we maintain a vigilant attitude, we may have the same thing happen to us today. And confusion will result.

We must learn to establish priorities in our thoughts as well as in our affairs. When we learn to put the most important things first, we will find that a pattern of order begins to emerge.

Strangely enough, as we refuse those inconsequential matters entrance into our minds, they will go away and seek a home where they are more welcome. They won't bother us any more.

Don't give the material things first place in your life.

The prophet Hosea accused the Israelites of making gods of the works of their hands. He pointed out that they were depending on materialistic strength, rather than turning to God for spiritual support and guidance. As a natural result, they were in difficulties—another example of confusion in mind, followed by confusion in affairs.

Hosea also referred to their trust in Assyria, which has an interesting meaning for us.

Assyria stands for *the reasonings, philosophical and psychical, that do not recognize the spiritual Head of the universe, but are based upon sense observation, upon the formed instead of the formless.* When we depend on the reasoning power of our minds, we are very likely to base our thoughts on material considerations only; and when we do this, we are subject to the material conditions around us and, hence, to confused conditions.

Limitation is characteristic of the material world and also of the reasoning power of mind that deals with material things. But when we learn to look to God first, as Hosea exhorted the people to do, we find that the limitations fade away, and the plagues and hardships that held us in bondage disappear as well. We can clear up confusion!

Do go within, where the answer lies.

We will never find answers where the confusion lies. We can never see the way through a maze by beating on the brick walls. We have to retire from the whole situation, whether it is mental or material in form, in order to renew ourselves and to revamp our whole viewpoint.

Remembering that confusion has no power over us unless we accept it in mind, we must cleanse in mind the symptoms or false reports of the confused state of mind. Then we are ready to proceed under God's direction. We can't hold in mind both God and problems. If we insist on staying with the problem, we automatically shut God out.

The trouble or confusion may be very obvious to the human reasoning or the physical senses, but regardless of the appearances, regardless of past experience, regardless of the feeling of complete disorder, there is only one place where we can receive the answer we need, and that is within ourselves. We must completely withdraw from the situation in order to find our way through.

Many scientists have spent years trying to find the answer to a particular problem. They may be trying to break some secret code of nature or come up with a new invention, and they try everything the human reasoning mind can suggest. Feeling that there is an answer, they may become frustrated and confused, wondering what to do next. And, more than once, one of these sincere seekers has given up in exhaustion, laid down to sleep, and received the answer either in a dream or in a clear revelation, sometimes in the form of a mental picture. The answer is there, but when we continue to force and push and seek it according to the world's way, we only succeed in becoming more and more frustrated. By withdrawing from the world, we find each answer where it always lives, within us.

Do speak the language of spirituality.

In the aims and goals of the world, there is always self-interest, and there are always conflict and dissension, frustration and confusion. But when we learn to leave behind the language of materiality, with all of its pitfalls and limitations, we can learn a new means of communication with our good, the language of spirituality.

Much confusion is the result of a conflict of interest, but there is no conflict when we seek the Truth, when we hold fast to that which is right and good, regardless of appearances.

God is greater than error. His presence is higher than confusion. His ways are above and beyond the materialism of the multitude.

There may be times when confusion is around us. There may be occasions when wrong seems to triumph in our world. There may even be times when we become temporarily lost in the maze of our minds, with their wonderings and wanderings.

But, if we will earnestly and sincerely seek God's answer, if we truly desire to speak the language of spirituality, we will learn how. We will find that beyond all false appearances and in spite of negation and wrong in our world,

God is good, and God is greater. When we speak the language of spirituality in all our thoughts, words, and actions, then we will no longer allow ourselves to be disturbed by those mirages of confusion. And we will create a world that will express the ideals of Spirit.

How to Succeed Every Time

Nothing is too good for you as a child of God!

When you realize this completely, you will be ready to claim all your heart's desires. Before you have asked, God has provided for you, His beloved offspring, the health, wealth, and unlimited success of the universe.

Even though you have asked very little of life and settled for less, it is not too late! When you begin to accept the promise of your rich heritage, you are on your way to becoming successful in everything you undertake, whether it is the overcoming of some bad habit, the healing of a physical difficulty, or the achieving of a lifelong goal.

The Bible is full of success stories. Many people became leaders of multitudes and achieved great wealth and power. Others found healing and answers to their problems. Still others learned to make that all-important contact with the "still small voice" within and were thus able to accomplish whatever was required of them as God's channels.

You too can be successful in whatever you want to undertake. You can, if you will learn the principles of success and work with them in your life. You can be healed. You can achieve business success. You can have prosperity beyond your greatest dreams.

As children of God, we are not to think small. We are to expand our thoughts and our dreams out into the universe and draw forth all the good we need to express God's abundance, whether it is abundance of health, joy, and peace, or the abundance of the world's goods that we need to live richly and share with others.

Many times people feel that if they had lived at other times and in other places they would have been successful. But they fail to see that the spirit of success is universal and imminent. It is just as available to us today as it ever was, and it does not depend on time or place or other people.

Countless individuals feel that if they could have known Jesus Christ, could have followed Him or just approached Him once, they could have been healed. They look at the instantaneous healings, the stories that are told over and over, and wish they could have been there.

Such a person was the woman who touched the hem of Jesus' garment and was immediately healed of a difficulty that had plagued her for years. But there was something different about this woman, something that those who envy her may have missed. She believed. She was in tune. Had she not been transformed from within, had she not been prayerfully aware of the stirring of the life force within her, she could not have been receptive even to the great flow of healing activity that Jesus projected. She had done her homework! When she was ready, her contact with Jesus brought about the result as the culmination of her faith and work. The healing came about because she was ready for it—inside.

A less familiar story from the life of Jesus is the incident with the blind man. This incident carries its own special message, one that is essential to any person who would be truly successful. With the woman, the results were instantaneous because she was ready. With the blind man, it took a little longer.

When this man was brought to Jesus by his friends, Jesus gave him quite a complicated healing treatment. He took the man's hand and led him out of the village, then He . . . *spit on his eyes and laid his hands upon him.* (Mark 8:23) Even this was not enough. The man reported: *"I see men; but they look like trees, walking."* (Mark 8:24) Progress had been made, and light was penetrating his dark world, but the healing was by no means complete. Why? Something more was needed.

After Jesus had given him a second healing treatment, the man was able to see everything clearly.

Sometimes our demonstrations come like that. We may have to persist all the way through to achieve the good we truly desire. Our answer may not come forth as quickly as we would like. But, when we are ready, we may be sure that the good will appear. Persistence is a quality of the successful person, and it is a requirement in all prayer treatment.

Other stories in the Bible also illustrate this. God has given us the deep desires of our hearts, and the desire within us for spiritual growth, greater abundance, healing, or successful participation in life is the promise that the answer is ours. Sometimes the promise is in the form of deliverance from a particular challenge that confronts us, something that seems to keep us from our good.

Consider the story of the battle between the Israelites and the Amalekites (descendants of

Esau) in the wilderness.

The people of Amalek had been harrassing the children of Israel as they traveled. It was their habit to strike at the stragglers, picking off those who were weak, feeble, weary, or faint— the ones who lagged behind the multitude. Their inroads became so great that Moses realized it would be necessary to fight.

As the spiritual leader of the group, he instructed Joshua to choose men and prepare for battle. He, on the other hand, would stand on a hilltop nearby, holding the rod of God high. This rod was an ordinary shepherd's crook, but it represented spiritual power to Moses and to the people, for it had been used in many miracles.

All went according to plan. The Israelites, under Joshua's leadership, were winning the battle. Then Moses' arms began to get tired, and the situation changed. According to the writer of Exodus: *Whenever Moses held up his hand, Israel prevailed; and whenever he lowered his hand, Amalek prevailed.* (Exod. 17:11)

Finally, a solution was found. Moses sat down on a stone, and Aaron and Hur, his brother and brother-in-law, assisted him, one on each side, holding up his arms *so his hands were steady until the going down of the sun.* (Exod. 17:12) With the rod representing spiritual power held high and in clear sight, the Israelites prevailed in the battle. Their prayer was answered, and they were delivered from the Amalekites. They were successful.

This is not only a story of answered prayer, but it is also a symbolic instruction in success thinking for us.

As in all metaphysical interpretation of Bible stories, the people stand for our thoughts, and the land represents the consciousness.

The Amalekites are thoughts of selfishness, self-indulgence, doubt, and fear. They live in the valley—*that great realm of mind called the subconscious.* From there, they come out to attack our thinking whenever we are weak or weary or disturbed (the stragglers, the weakest part of the company). The Israelites represent *the illumined thoughts in consciousness, which are undergoing spiritual discipline.* But these thoughts, while they are trying to follow divine law, are by no means perfect yet, and they have their weak links. These wandering thoughts are most vulnerable to false concepts of selfishness, self-indulgence, doubt, and fear.

When we are aware that our spiritual aims and goals are being undermined by these negative dwellers in our subconscious minds, then it is time to put Moses in charge and get rid of the Amalekites.

Moses represents the understanding of God as law, and it is his job to lead the undisciplined thoughts through the wilderness of false thinking to their fulfillment as divine ideas in our minds.

In this case, he takes charge by sending Joshua (the unfolding realization of the I AM or Christ power within) to vanquish the Amalekites, while he, the law, maintains a high spiritual consciousness (holds the rod on high). But understanding of God as the law isn't enough to maintain the God realization that is necessary to wipe out all those invaders from the subconscious mind—those thought-people that whisper of discouragement and fear of failure.

So Moses has to have assistance from his brother Aaron, and his brother-in-law Hur. Aaron always works very closely with his brother. He, as the will or executive power of the mind, must back up the understanding of God as law. On the other side, Hur stands strong as affirmative prayer. So, with the help of the will, rightly directed, and strong affirmations, we are able to maintain the high spiritual awareness that carries us all the way through to victory over those sneaky invaders, the Amalekites. We are thus able to continue our progress toward greater and greater success in living.

Again, it takes persistence! If we allow our

faith in God to flag, if we let ourselves become easily discouraged and weary with trying, we lose our grip on life and living, and we begin to lose the battle. So we can't really afford to give up, no matter how things seem to be going "down below." Instead, we enlist those powers of will and affirmative prayer and work our way through the situation to victory.

This story gives us some instructions for successful living that apply today.

Don't give up.

How many times people start out with high hopes, seeking to solve problems or improve conditions in their lives through spiritual methods and prayer activity. Then they revert to old ways of thinking, letting the old habits pick off those lagging hopes and dreams, the ones that haven't yet attained full maturity in their minds.

They may become so taken up with the problems and the seeming impossibility of succeeding that they give up, blaming God for their own shortcomings, saying, "God didn't answer my prayer." God always answers our prayer; and, if it seems that the answer is long in coming, perhaps it is because we are letting down in our spiritual activity. Perhaps it is time to enlist affirmative prayer and the will to carry on as we continue to lift up the rod of God (maintain the spiritual activity, regardless of appearances). When we are ready, the answer will come; and it may be greater than anything we expected in our earlier state of understanding.

Many times, people with whom we have counseled come back and report, "You know that prayer you gave me? I said it twenty-five times and nothing happened!" Then we must explain that it isn't "saying" a prayer that gets results. We must reach the inner realization that is ready for the answer, ready to receive the success that awaits each of us as the children of God that we are.

Then there is another question we must ask those who feel their prayers haven't been answered. And that is: how do you know your prayer wasn't answered? Perhaps you have sought physical evidence of the answer when you should have been sticking with the realization of the answer. It may take time for the success to show in your life; but once you have completed the necessary God-contact, you can leave it up to God to determine the time and place for the results to show, while you keep up your spiritual work, even if you must stand tall and affirm God's good all the way *until the going down of the sun.*

Perhaps the area in which you want to be

successful is sticking to a diet to lose weight. Here too God can help you. Before you start the diet, know that God is greater than even the most powerful craving for self-indulgence (one of those sneaky Amalekites from the subconscious mind).

When discouragement says, "You aren't really making any progress," and the low thought urges, "Oh, go ahead and eat that piece of cake," it's time to call on Aaron and Hur. With the help of the will backing up your understanding, and prayer affirmations getting your attention back on positive ideas, you can overcome; and in the long run you will be successful.

You will never know how close you are to success if you simply surrender—give up to those negative invaders.

Remember, you do not give up to the Amalekites in your mind, and you can't win simply by fighting them down in the valley. It is on the hilltop where the air is clear and your thoughts are uplifted that you win the battle. Then the outer condition expresses the overcoming you have made within yourself.

Do accept God's encouragement.

Along the way, we may have evidences that we are progressing, that we are becoming stronger and better able to achieve and to overcome. But, here again, we must beware of the Amalekites. They may invade our thinking with such strong feelings of doubt and fear that, instead of recognizing the little signs of progress, we revert to old concepts of failure and discouragement.

Perhaps we haven't had the great success we have sought. Maybe we haven't experienced the healing that was so important. But, if we have earnestly and sincerely held up the rod of God, refusing to give up and continuing with our affirmations of God's power and activity, then something has happened!

Many times, while praying for healing of a particular condition, individuals have suddenly discovered that smaller, less deeply-rooted states have been harmonized. If you have been praying for the healing of something as serious as a cancerous condition and find that a sty on your eye or a mole on your chin has been removed, then give thanks for the healing.

Don't look at the longtime difficulty and complain because it hasn't been corrected. Instead, give thanks for God's encouragement, the sign that you are tuning in to the healing idea. Then keep your vision high until the larger result is achieved.

Perhaps you are working toward some tremendous goal in your personal or professional life, and that big result seems to elude you. Don't give up. As you look around, you may be surprised at the number of "small miracles" taking place in your life. Even something as simple as finding the perfect parking place is a sign that you are tuning in to spiritual power. Look at the answers you are receiving, give thanks for them, and let them reinforce your determination to keep your "rod of God" as high as you can hold it with the help of understanding, will, and affirmative prayer.

Do persist all the way through.

The greatest achievements require a great investment, and the most important resource that we can invest is ourselves. Actually, we are giving ourselves to life all the time anyway. But what are we giving?

If we let those low thoughts of fear, doubt, and self-indulgence take over, we are investing ourselves in failure, letting the invaders choke our spiritual aspirations as they arise. And we will get back our failure thoughts with interest. Life pays us in the coin of our thinking.

Only we can choose to invest ourselves in high ideals and aspirations, spiritual aims and goals, visions of ourselves as joyous, free, and successful. Only we can stop those Amalekites when they come out of the valley, eradicating them completely from our minds as we stand on the high places of spiritual vision and positive, powerful prayers.

This is not a one-time process. It is a continuing process in spiritual living, a journey that takes us all the way through the wilderness experiences of living into the promised land of abundance.

If we do give in to weakness and discouragement, if we fall by the wayside in our ongoing, even then we don't have to settle for failure. The Moses of our nature waits, ready to lift us up into the awareness that, by working with God as law all the way through, we will truly reap the rewards of the kingdom.

We are designed for success—in healing, in overcoming, and in living. We are created to triumph over all limitations that can arise in our daily experiences; and we begin this triumphant living by conquering the Amalekites in our minds.

We are supposed to be successful in our chosen work. We are to excel in the areas in which we choose to express. We are to be that which we are designed to be—the perfect expression of spiritual Truth. And we will succeed every time when we put God first, lifting our thoughts and our vision, our understanding and our will to the dream of fulfillment He has placed in our hearts.

Printed U.S.A.

155-F-5223-15M-2-82